AUSTRALIA

Commonwealth History

Editor
SIR REGINALD COUPLAND
KCMG, CIE, MA, D.LITT
late Beit Professor of History of the British Empire
in the University of Oxford

AUSTRALIA

R. M. Crawford
Formerly Professor of History
in the University of Melbourne

HUTCHINSON UNIVERSITY LIBRARY
LONDON

HUTCHINSON & CO (*Publishers*) LTD
178–202 Great Portland Street, London W1

London Melbourne Sydney
Auckland Johannesburg Cape Town
and agencies throughout the world

First published 1952
Reprinted 1955, 1957, 1958, 1960
Second edition 1960
Reprinted 1961, 1963, 1965, 1968
Third (revised) edition 1970

This book has been set in Times type, printed in Great Britain
on smooth wove paper by Anchor Press, and
bound by Wm. Brendon, both of Tiptree, Essex

ISBN 0 09 105110 X (cased)
0 09 105111 8 (paper)

CONTENTS

MAPS

NOTE TO THE THIRD EDITION

Since this book was first published, Australia has been changed in many ways. Those changes have been accompanied by a reassessment of Australia's past history no less profound. I have therefore been obliged not only to bring Chapter 11 up-to-date, but to take account of the main directions of recent research. My debt to this work is made clear in the text. To the acknowledgment of the first edition, I add my grateful thanks to many colleagues who have helped me, and above all to my wife, both for her particular knowledge of the history of social welfare and for general encouragement.

The University of Melbourne   R.M.C.

NOTE TO THE FIRST EDITION

I wish to acknowledge the kind permission of the Meanjin Press, Melbourne, to quote Judith Wright's poems 'Remittance Man' and 'The Bullocky' from *The Moving Image* (Melbourne) and of the Melbourne University Press to quote A. D. Hope's poem 'Australia' from *Modern Australian Poetry* (1946). With the permission of their authors, I have made extensive use of three unpublished theses in the library of the University of Melbourne—Mr F. K. Crowley's *History of Working-Class Conditions in Australia*, 1788–1850, Mr G. H. Nadel's *Mid-Nineteenth Century Thought in New South Wales and Victoria*, and Mr S. M. Ingham's *Some Aspects of Victorian Parliamentary Liberalism*, 1880–1900. I have received help from more colleagues than I can name. To Miss Kiddle for her digging on my behalf, to Mr A. Wilcock for his maps, to Miss I. Wilcock for correcting the manuscript, and to the many others with whom I discussed problems ranging from breeds of wheat to economic theory, I give my thanks. I have been helped beyond acknowledgment by Associate-Professor Kathleen Fitzpatrick who has aided this book with a wise blue pencil and with patience.

The University of Melbourne.   R.M.C.

I

THE LAND

The history of Australia is a chapter in the history of migration. Until comparatively recent times, the great majority of its European inhabitants had come to it from elsewhere. Not until 1870 did the native-born outnumber those who had come from the old world. The seven seas may divide the migrant from his homeland, but he will never quite shake its dust from his feet. Colonial settlements were not, therefore, completely new communities beginning from nothing. Their people brought with them much invisible luggage, the known ways and the familiar ideas and institutions of another world.

Nor did these new settlements grow in isolation; their growth depended in many ways on the changing state of things in Great Britain and Europe, a state of things over which they had little or no control but which they might on occasion use to their advantage. It was the growth of Britain's population and her economic revolution that provided the migrants, both free and unfree, who settled this country. It was the industrial revolution which created the demand for all the fine wool Australia could supply and the capital which fed the expansion of Australia's pastoral industry. In these and in many other ways yet to be told, Australia's growth responded step by step to developments in the old world.

Nevertheless, to migrate is to be uprooted, to be compelled to adjust old habits and assumptions to new circumstances. Because the circumstances are different from those of the homeland, one finds in all colonial societies a mixture of conservative habit and innovation. For where the new condition does not force adjustment, the migrant clings to his accustomed ways with all the force of the exile, even though those same ways may have grown old-fashioned with the passing times in his former home. But this nostalgic conservative must also be an improvisor, to meet the challenge of unfamiliar conditions.

The most unfamiliar condition that confronted our forefathers was the land itself. Even had they come from lands of similar latitude and similar climate in the northern hemisphere, from Spain, Morocco, Libya and Arabia, they must still have found the southern continent strange for its trees and animals that were unknown to Europe. But the major physical condition affecting occupation of Australia is its dryness; and that would have been a familiar tale to our imagined—and historically impossible—settlers from Spain, North Africa and Arabia. In fact, Australia, which lies between latitudes 10 degrees and 43 degrees south, was settled by people coming from green, well-watered islands in latitudes 50 degrees to 60 degrees north, and for them the bridge of adaptation was wide indeed.

The greater part of Australia lies in the warm dry belt of latitude, in which the deserts of the world occur, such as the Sahara in the northern hemisphere, the Kalahari and Atacama deserts in the southern. Professor Gregory defines a desert as 'country with such an arid climate and such a scanty water supply that agriculture is impracticable and occupation is found possible only for a sparse population of pastoralists'. Outside the Antarctic, there is no desert in the southern hemisphere so extensive as the Australian, 600,000 square miles of it unused and unusable, and another 700,000 square miles good only for sparse pastoral occupation, in a total area of under 3,000,000 square miles.

For in these parallels, the air, up-drawn at the equator, is descending once more from very high altitudes and has lost much of its moisture as it approaches the earth. It brings moderate rains as an on-shore wind on the east coast of land masses, but quickly becomes a dry and drying wind as it moves westward over the land. Consequently the effect of Australia's position is doubled by its shape, as it stretches its greatest extent along the driest belt of latitude. The effect of this is clear in Professor Griffith Taylor's comparison of the westward march of early settlers in America and Australia. 'The Australian reached an arid environment rather like that of Arizona at 450 miles from the coast while the American in a similar journey was just reaching the beginning of the best section of the United States in Eastern Ohio.'

It is true that 40 per cent of Australia lies within the tropics, and its northern parts receive rains from the summer monsoon as the sun stands down towards Capricorn. Similarly, the southern extremities of Australia, both on the west and east, benefit from the winter rains as the sun retreats north of the equator, dragging the northern limit of the wet westerlies after it. Very roughly, one may divide Australia into three main sections as to rainfall—an eastern coastal section which receives some rain from on-shore winds throughout the year, a northern section of summer rain and a southern section of winter rains.

But the on-shore winds of the eastern coasts quickly lose their moisture as they move inland. The Australian tropics lie on the southern and uncertain fringe of summer rains which grow heavier and more regular as one crosses the straits to New Guinea. Tasmania and southern Victoria apart, the south coasts likewise lie on the northern and uncertain fringe of the winter rains, which grow heavier and more regular south of the fortieth parallel. Were Australia nearer the equator or nearer the pole, it would be wetter and more fertile than it is; in fact it sprawls along the driest belt of latitude.

Consequently Australia's rainfall is in almost all parts extremely unreliable, and the average annual rainfall declines rapidly as one moves inland. Indeed, in one area of Western Australia's forest country, the decline is one inch a mile, from forty inches on the coast to twenty inches only twenty miles inland. But the crude average of annual rainfall is a deceptive guide in considering land-use. The amount that would sustain crops in southern Australia would not be enough to do so in the hot dry north and centre, where the rate of evaporation of moisture from the earth's surface and vegetation is extremely high.

Most deceptive for those who would possess this country and use it are the extreme variations from year to year in the amount of rainfall. The dependence of Australia on the fringes of the summer and winter rainfall systems has given her rainfall its characteristic uncertainty which has brought defeat to many a would-be settler. What has seemed country of marvellous promise to explorer or venturing squatter or farmer in a good year has turned into forbidding desert in all too frequent bad years. Again and again in Australia's white history, settlers have been tempted out by the good year to learn the lesson of defeat in the inevitable years of drought. The converse is also true; sheep now graze, though sparsely, where the explorer Sturt and his party found utter desolation in the bad years, 1844 and 1845.

The result of these conditions is that Australia is in large part an arid country. Barely a quarter of it is wet enough for agriculture, and of that much is mountainous. Of the rest, about half is good pastoral land. The remainder is dry and sparse pastoral land or absolute desert.

The fact that vegetation of some sort clothes the greater part of the dry areas surprises and even misleads many people when they first see it. Indeed, arid Australia is for most Australians an area of report rather than of personal experience, for inevitably the vast majority of Australians live 'on the rim of the saucer', in the regions of better rainfall. To them, known Australia is the country of the gum-tree, the eucalypt. The still unnumbered varieties of this tree range from the tall mountain ash of Victoria and the karri of Western Australia to the squat mallee of the dry fringes of settlement, with its long roots reaching out in search of water. But over still larger areas of Australia, its really arid areas, the gum-tree is not dominant at all, but gives way to stretches of mulga or brigalow (low-growing acacias), or to plains where the gum-trees are hemmed back into the dry creek beds, and even the mulgas thin out, to stand isolated among the squat hummocks of salt bush and blue bush and the clumps of spinifex, grey and blue against the dominant red of the inland. This is the area of the limitless plains with their long slow rises to imperceptible elevations, and islanded in them the occasional hard bone of rock that has resisted long ages of weathering.

In the tropical areas there are pockets of jungle on the east coast of Queensland, less extensive than in days gone by, and in occasional river valleys around the north of Australia. But the normal vegetation of tropical Australia is thin savannah forest, fringed on coast and tidal river by mangrove swamps, and standing amidst the tall, tough and not very nutritious grasses whose rank growth follows the heavy and short summer rains of 'the Wet'.

For the visitor, as for the early settler, these long miles of seemingly sombre vegetation are often of an oppressive and melancholy monotony. But in time both immigrants and native sons were to learn the subtle beauties of the Australian bush—the grey-blue of distant ranges, the morning sun glistening on the narrow leaves of mulga and mallee, the slow contours of the plains. This new sight was quickened by the association of place and treasured memory, so that in time the white Australian could learn the love of his locality which was the aboriginal's before his displacement. But the sense of desolation that oppressed many early settlers in the gentler regions of Australia can still overtake even the Australian visitor to the ancient eroded desert between the centre and the north-west of Australia. 'The major portion of the country,' wrote one of them after a pioneer flight over this area, 'is so utterly desolate, arid, and dead, as to fill one with sadness.'

In temperature, Australia ranges from the cool temperate climate of its south-eastern extremity, Tasmania, to the extremely hot

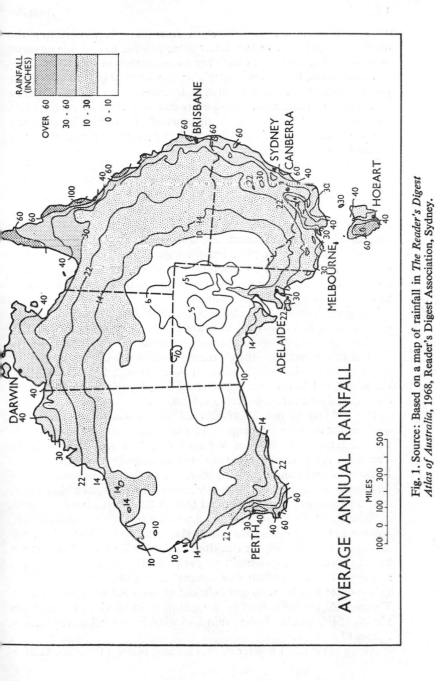

AVERAGE ANNUAL RAINFALL

Fig. 1. Source: Based on a map of rainfall in *The Reader's Digest Atlas of Australia*, 1968, Reader's Digest Association, Sydney.

climate of those parts of Western Australia which lie along the tropic of Capricorn. In this latter area, Marble Bar in one summer 'experienced 152 days in which the mean maximum was 109 degrees F.'. In general, though winter nights can be cold indeed over large parts of Australia, the continent is to be classed as from warm to hot. Even in Melbourne, where a fire can be a comfort occasionally on a December evening, it is an unusual summer which does not provide a scattering of days on which the temperature rises near or above 100 degrees F.

The physical conditions which the British settlers of Australia would need in time to learn may be further understood by a glimpse of some of the major effects of its geological history. The first of these is the deficiency of much of its soil, particularly in the western half of the continent. There are good soils in some of the dry areas, but, alluvial river flats apart, the soils of the agricultural areas are only of fair average quality. Experience and study were required to show their deficiences in calcium and phosphorus, and, in some areas, in the trace elements of copper and cobalt which are necessary to the health of plants and animals.

The great bulk of Australia forms one of the stable shields of the earth's crust. But Australia also lies in close proximity with one of the most unstable zones of the earth's surface, in which land and sea are still in the making—the extremely mobile belt curving round the north of Australia from south-east Asia through New Guinea and the Solomon Islands, and the less mobile belt running parallel to the east coast down through New Zealand.

The stability of the Australian shield has had important consequences for its human occupation. The area of greatest stability has been the northern part of Western Australia and the Northern Territory. No part of the earth's surface is more ancient than this. In its soils and metamorphic rocks, the geologist can read the unimaginably long story of the slow wearing down of a once high massif into a vast desert plateau about 1,000 to 1,500 feet above sea level.

Since a period of upheaval and alteration lost in the dawn of time, erosion has gone on, in this most stable section of the shield, unchecked by any folding or buckling of the earth's crust which might have formed young mountain ranges and set going a new process of soil deposition. It has no rivers except along the coast to build up valley soils; and its soils are deficient even by Australian standards. Through all the periods of geological time, in pluvial as well as dry phases of the land's history, rain and wind have worked together as agents of erosion.

Along the eastern border of this ancient plateau from the Gulf of

Carpentaria to the Murray River mouth there lies a vast trough. Here soil has been deposited on an extensive scale in Tertiary times, but in an area which is, outside the South Australian wheat belt, too dry for agriculture. Fortunately, much of this trough lies over Australia's greatest artesian basin; and artesian waters, too limited in quantity and in general too salty to nourish agriculture, have nevertheless increased the capacity of the area to carry sheep and cattle.

East again of this trough, one ascends gradually towards the long spine of mountains which forms the Great Dividing Range and runs from North Queensland south into Victoria. These were probably elevated in Palaeozoic times by pressure on the shield from the unstable areas of the earth's crust to the east of Australia; and they are steep and rugged on the east, the side of pressure, while they slope gently into table-lands on the west. They make up a considerable proportion of Australia's well-watered belt, and reduce the area useful for agriculture. Although these mountains are not high, reaching their greatest height of 7,328 feet at Kosciusko in the south-eastern Alps, they contain some of Australia's most majestic scenery, whether in the upthrust blocks of the Blue Mountains west of Sydney, or in the folded contours of the Alps of southern New South Wales and eastern Victoria, so smoothly rounded by volcanic and glacial action.

Too rugged for agricultural use except for their western slopes, these mountains serve as catchment areas, to supply water for consumption, irrigation and power. It is an oddity of the Australian topography that its tallest mountains are under the sea, where the Tasmantides, 150 miles east of south Queensland, rise 16,000 feet above the ocean bed to within 500 feet of the surface. But the mountains above water are too low to support extensive and permanent snow-fields, and the quantity of water from this source is limited, even in Victoria and Tasmania. The greatest potential sources of hydro-electric power in Australia and its territories are in the island of New Guinea, with its tall mountains and heavy rainfall, and—a long way second—the island of Tasmania with a regular rainfall supplemented by winter snow. Next to these come the Australian Alps of southern New South Wales and Victoria, where rainfall also is in minor degree supplemented by winter snows. The amount of water available from these continental sources is not enough to meet likely demands for power or to irrigate all the areas that are economically worth irrigating.

East again of the Dividing Range is the coastal plain where land and sea remain in unresolved conflict. The sinking of river valleys has created much magnificent scenery and some fine harbours. Running parallel to the Queensland coast from Cape York down to Rockhampton is the extensive area of coral known as the Great Barrier Reef.

The legacy of long ages of geological change is a land, for the most part very ancient, tied to south-east Asia by a string of islands, severed from it by the straits and passages between those islands. The straits have not prevented the migration of Malayan flora into parts of tropical Australia, nor did they prevent the crossing of men. But the great ocean deeps of the Sunda Straits shielded the Australian marsupials from the carnivorous animals of Asia, and preserved Australia as a biological museum of earlier forms.

In a continent which ranges from a tropical to a cool temperate climate, there is considerable variety; but this variety is so thinly spaced out over vast distances that it is less readily evident than an appearance of sameness. Indeed, in all the diversity of the country there is a homogeneity which makes one aware, in all parts of the mainland at least, that it is Australian. The clear brilliant light of these latitudes, with its effect on distance, tone and colour; the ancient, hard-weathered land forms; and the similarities in difference of vegetation; all contribute to this sense of uniformity.

From the savannah woodlands of the tropical north to the tall and dense eucalypt forests of the east coasts and southern corners, thinning out into low-growing mallee and mulga inland, unlikeness is bridged by likeness. In all parts, there is the dominance of trees that keep their leaves which are so commonly long, narrow and pendant; the sparseness of foliage compared with the prominence of trunk and bough and twig; the blues and greys and reddish browns of this vegetation that stand in sharp contrast with the lush green of European trees; and, over all, the hard clear light of the southern day.

Through the long ages of Australia's isolation from the rest of the world, a delicate balance of soil and vegetation and animal life was evolved, and remained undisturbed by the food-gathering and food-hunting aborigines, who lived in the land by adapting themselves to its ways. So the land lay, unknown to Europeans and little visited by Asians, through long centuries while the empires of Europe and Asia rose and fell.

2

THE ABORIGINES

When this book was first written, it was not possible to say how long the aborigines had lived in Australia before the coming of Europeans. There was some presumptive evidence for the presence of man on the continent in late Pleistocene times, his migrations being assisted in the most recent glacial phases by the lowering of sea levels and the narrowing of the water barriers in his path.

The rapid growth in recent years of archaeological research assisted by the advent of Carbon–14 dating has given us dates of occupation in excess of 20,000 years before the present, and dates of 30,000 years and more may now be confidently expected. Many of the most ancient sites must today lie under the sea, as they were occupied when the continental shelf surrounding the present coasts of north-western and northern Australia was dry land.

Within the time-span of twenty or thirty thousand years, archaeologists have discerned changes in material culture the full significance of which remains speculative. From about 5,000 years ago there was added to the simple core and flake industry of preceding millenia (an industry which nevertheless persisted into modern times) a much more sophisticated point and blade technology. This 'Inventive Phase' merged into an 'Adaptive Phase' (to use Mr J. Mulvaney's terminology, *The Prehistory of Australia,* 1969) in which inventive variety gave way to a measure of simplification.

Were these changes made by the same peoples or did they mark waves of migration?

Physical anthropologists meanwhile are examining skeletal remains with similar questions in mind. The marked differences between 'primitive' skills such as the Talgai skull and 'modern' skulls such as the Keilor skull, which may nevertheless be 15,000 years old, have suggested a very early mingling of races. Such mingling may have taken place in Australia; it may also have taken place along the routes of migration.

It is certain that man came to Australia from elsewhere and had to cross open water to do so. In the long distant past Australia was probably connected with Asiatic land masses and at that time received its primitive animals such as monotremes and marsupials. But it was separated from other land masses before the higher mammals such as cats, deer, rabbits and monkeys had arrived in southern Asia; and consequently before the appearance of homo sapiens.

Even when the continental shelf was exposed by the lowering of levels during glacial periods, our aboriginal immigrants must have had to cross such deep-water spaces as Wallace's Line between Borneo and Celebes, Bali and Lombok, or the sea between Timor and the Sahul Shelf if they followed that route. Successive groups probably landed at various points in Northern Australia from Cape York to the Kimberleys, spread round the northern and down both western and eastern coasts, and inland along the river systems. Almost certainly they brought their native dog, the dingo, with them.

In modern times, there were obvious physical differences between the mainland and Tasmanian aborigines. The latter were a negroid type, frizzy haired where the Australians are straight or wavy haired, and generally darker skinned than their neighbours of the mainland. While both Tasmanians and Australians were semi-nomadic food-gathering and food-hunting peoples, the material culture of the Tasmanians was less advanced than that of the mainland. They had neither boomerang nor spearthrower; and as to stone implements, they lacked the more advanced types, the pressure-flaked, ground and polished implements which, on the mainland, were used together with more primitive types resembling the Tasmanian.

The comparative primitiveness of their material culture does not necessarily imply a crude social organization; for study of the mainland tribes has shown that among them there is no regular correlation between varying levels of material culture and the complexity of social structure and behaviour. We simply do not know enough about the extinct culture of the Tasmanians to come to general conclusions about it. Their derivation must also remain a matter for speculation, and there is as yet no conclusive evidence to decide between those who believe that the first Tasmanians drifted ashore from the Pacific and those who see them as the island remnants of a mainland people absorbed by other peoples on the mainland. Tasmania's oldest sites must lie under the sea of Bass Strait. So far, Tasmanian sites have been dated no further back than 8,000 years ago, and even within this relatively short period Mr Rhys Jones has found a change from people living from the sea to people seeking their food from the land.

Although modern occupation destroys archaeological evidence, enough remains to give archaeologists rich opportunities in the future. But time is running out for anthropological enquiry. Already, before scientific anthropological work had been organized, the last full-blooded Tasmanian had died in 1876 and the Victorian tribes were virtually no more. Even where full-blooded aborigines survived in considerable number, much of their lore had gone for ever; for the old men, its guardians, had with sorrow refrained from passing on their secret and sacred knowledge to detribalized younger men whom they considered unworthy of it. Today, only a handful of aborigines still live in a fully tribal state and there are virtually none who have not had recurrent contact with white men.

Systematic study of tribal aborigines was stepped up in the 1920s and 1930s with the support of the Australian National Research Council and greatly intensified in the 1960s by the establishment of the Australian Institute of Aboriginal Studies. There is much that can never be known, but more is known now than ever before. What follows can be no more than a sketch, allowing nothing for the variations from people to people and from time to time.

Aboriginal traditions do not speak of ancient migrations from distant places, though they are full of the wanderings within Australia of totemic ancestors. In general, these ancestors are believed to have emerged in an ancient 'dream-time' from a dormant state into a period of activity. In some cases they received life from supernatural beings who came down to earth and set free their limbs and opened their eyes and mouths. In others, the ancestors simply stirred into life of themselves in their resting places beneath some soak or water-hole, and rose to the surface of the earth; while the long unbroken darkness was scattered and the featureless landscape was filled with life.

Each ancestor, whether male of female, is associated with a totem, a member of the plant or animal kingdoms such as the yam, witchet-ty grub, bandicoot or kangaroo, or even with a natural feature such as a particular wind or the sky. From them sprang children, and the animals or plants of their totem, the former thought of as human beings but also at times as the totemic plant or animal endowed with human characteristics.

The most intricate series of adventures followed as the ancestors roamed the land, as readily beneath its surface as upon it. The legends reflect a time of great violence, of war between father and sons and between the various totemic groups. In the course of their

wanderings, their fighting and their love-making, these ancestors
created the various natural features of the tribal territory—its hills,
its gorges and its rivers, heaps of boulders, even ancient trees.
Moreover, they were culture heroes who taught the material culture,
the knowledge and use of natural resources, and the sacred lore of
the tribe.

In the course of time, they sank back, not into death, though they
might appear to be slain, but into quiescence. Something of their
vital activity remained, in places at which they had rested or in
objects thought of as their transformed bodies—a great boulder,
perhaps, or a tjurunga.

Tjurunga are sacred objects of wood or stone. They vary greatly
in size, from a few inches to six feet long; and in shape, from round
to an elongated oval. They are most commonly engraved with
geometrical designs emblematic, or rather, mnemonic, of the totem.
Some evidence has recently been discovered which suggests that the
designs of some earlier tjurunga may have represented the ancestors
more naturalistically. Whatever its design, the tjurunga associated
with a totemic ancestor is far more than emblematic; for it has the
mana—the spiritual power and virtue—of the living ancestor himself,
and may even be regarded as the transformed body of the ancestor.

Through hallowed tradition, as interpreted by the old men, the
totemic ancestors continued to govern the tribe. Indeed, by means of
their continuing procreative vitality, they quite literally gave it life.
For they were regarded as the progenitors, not only of those first
children who sprang fully grown from them, but also of every
succeeding generation.

It is still a matter of debate how far the facts of physical paternity
were known to the Australian native. The role of the human father
was thought of, if at all, as at most secondary; and the child that
grew in the mother's body was regarded as a spirit child of a totemic
ancestor who had entered her womb as she passed by some place
where the spirit children inhabited—some place where the particular
ancestor had rested during his wanderings, the boulders which
represented his sleeping body, or even, perhaps, the place of his
first emergence from the earth.

This belief stood, together with the natural difficulties of this
continent, in the way of any native development of agriculture. A
land which contained no animals which could be domesticated and
no plants which have anywhere been cultivated as crops, did not in
any case favour the discovery of farming; but native belief was a
further barrier against even the most limited attempts to increase by
cultivation the natural growth of their food-plants.

The natives of Australia have a wide range of vegetable as well as animal foods, and a detailed and accurate knowledge of the varieties, habits, and properties of these foods. As food gatherers and hunters, they are highly skilled and ingenious. They did all in their power to keep up the rate of reproduction of the plants and animals on which they depended; but their method of ensuring an adequate food supply was the method of ritual and not of cultivation.

For this purpose, increase ceremonies were practised at certain sites, such as a boulder or heap of stones held to be the transformed body of a totemic ancestor where the spirits of the plants or animals associated with him awaited incarnation. His life-engendering properties resided in the stone. By appropriate ritual, accompanied by action—such as rubbing the stone, blowing dust from it into the air, or taking from it powdered stone or earth mixed with blood to places where increase of game or plants was desired—the vital properties of the stone were scattered abroad to multiply the chances of increase of the species.

The ancestors, then, governed the living tribe in all aspects of its life. They were its direct progenitors in every generation, and the progenitors of the plants and animals on whom its life depended. They were the source of its material culture, the authors of its rituals, and in many cases the givers of its intricate social law.

Of all this knowledge, the respected guardians were the old men. Material culture and knowledge of nature the child picked up by observation, imitation, and teaching. So, too, by imperceptible degrees, he came to know the intricate kinship system, and the duties and the tabus that he must observe. But a great part of tribal law and legend was secret, to be made known only to adult males. Some of it was revealed to youths at the various stages of their initiation into manhood; but the more secret legends and rituals were imparted by their guardians only in the slow course of time, and then only to those who, by increasing maturity, worthiness, or personal totem, appeared to them fit to become in their turn the guardians of such knowledge. And so a man could grow in knowledge of tribal lore through all the years of his middle age; and always it was the older men who possessed the fullest knowledge of the traditions which governed the whole life of the tribe, and who held, therefore, the highest authority over it.

The rule of tradition as interpreted by the old men is the distinctive feature in the government of the Australian aborigines. In areas that remained exposed to outside influences, such as the coasts of Arnhem Land visited by Macassar seamen in search of bêche-de-mer, there is evidence that new customs and new beliefs could be adopted by the tribal natives; but only in so far as it proved possible to graft them on to old tradition and to give them the sanction and sanctity of ancient command. And the varying distribution of certain customs suggests a comparatively recent adoption of those which were less widespread, and an unfinished diffusion of them down from the northern coasts of Australia. For the area in which subincision was practised is contained within the area of circumcision; and both customs were less widespread than the knocking out of teeth at initiation.

In recent times, tradition had become fixed in inland areas remote from the Indonesian and Papuan influence which for centuries was the only external influence on Australian life. Established tradition gave certainty and security, but robbed the natives of invention and initiative.

In his *Aranda Traditions* Dr Strehlow points out that in Central Australia every feature of the landscape was long ago made the subject of legend, and the thoroughness of their forefathers had left the natives of a later day

not a single unoccupied scene which they could fill with the creatures of their own imagination. Tradition and the tyranny of the old men in the religious and cultural sphere have effectually stifled all creative impulse; and no external stimulus ever reached Central Australia which could have freed the natives from these insidious bonds. It is almost certain that native myths had ceased to be invented many centuries ago. . . . The present-day natives are on the whole merely the painstaking, uninspired preservers of a great and interesting inheritance. They live almost entirely on the traditions of their forefathers. They are in many ways, not so much a primitive, as a decadent race.

But Dr Strehlow shows in this same work, in common with other anthropologists, the obverse of this picture—the security, the social cohesion, and the support to personality that tradition gave. The authority of tradition was not simply that of the old men; it was that of the totemic ancestors, the most ancient and yet still living, still procreative culture heroes.

As on ceremonial occasion the young male initiates were led by their elders, up some winding mountain path or through the mulga scrub, to a secret storehouse in a cave or mulga stump which concealed the sacred objects, they listened to the old chants which enshrined the sacred myths and to their elders' interpretation of words so archaic as to be no longer understood without explanation. In reverent silence but memorizing their new knowledge, they were led into the presence of the tjurunga, which were to them, not merely the symbols of their ancestors, but even in some cases the very bodies of their ancestors, from which life and spiritual power still radiated. From such ceremonials they learnt the lore of the tribe and they gained a sense of their personal place in its continuing life from ancient times. Their growth in knowledge was accompanied by the wild excitement of dance and chant amid the whirling of bull-roarers, and even the bloodier excitements—the knocking out of teeth or the cutting of cicatrices; circumcision and recurrent subin-cision—which, having their place in tradition and social usage, were followed by a sense of release, of spiritual refreshment, and the security of belonging in some fuller sense to the community.

The fullest satisfaction of this kind was reserved to the men. The women had their own duties, and, in a limited sense, their own rituals and their own lore; and they shared in those legends and rituals which were not secret. But they were never admitted beyond the fringes of the sacred cults. They had their known place in tribal life; but it was a subordinate place. Where the men were the hunters, they were the gatherers of vegetable foods or at most hunters of very small game. They cared for the children until puberty, when the girls were married and the boys taken from their mothers into the control of the male guardians of their initiation. In the choice of husband they had no share, for marriage was governed by tribal custom interpreted by the older men.

But revolt against this dependence has been rare among natives still in a tribal state. Having no idea of self-assertion, they did not set ideals of independence against their actual lot. They, too, in more limited degree, felt security in the known ways of the tribe, though their share in its life was subordinate. Their capacity for enjoyment has been generally remarked by white observers.

The early settlers were naturally conscious of the externals of primitiveness of aboriginal life—the dirt and mortality, stone-age weapons, and lack of permanent shelters or agriculture. But modern study has shown that the aborigines had also achieved, by means of their traditions and rituals, a harmonious adjustment to a difficult natural environment, and a social cohesion and security which civilized man in an unsettled age of the world's history may grow a little wistful in describing.

Perhaps this adjustment is most striking in the relation of the aboriginal with his tribal territory. As food gatherers and hunters, the aborigines were of necessity wanderers. But they were in no extensive sense nomadic; for each group—tribe or clan—had its own recognized territory, large in the dry inland, much smaller in the wetter coastal areas, within which for the most part it lived its life.

As the wanderings of the totemic ancestors were not confined to tribal areas, ceremonies connected with ancestral tradition were often the occasion for the meeting of members of more than one tribe who had in common some association with the totem. Such excursions outside the tribal territory to a ceremonial site were governed by invitation and appropriate ceremony. There were other excursions less friendly, when expeditions of revenge sought a man who had abducted a woman of the tribe or who was regarded as responsible for the death of a tribal member; for in some areas, as in the Kimberleys, death was never regarded as natural, but always as a result of human agency employing a remote magic.

The native who went outside his own territory, except as invited guest, left security behind him. Not only were his motives necessarily suspect; he was in a land of spirits strange to him and in a place where he was ignorant of the appropriate rituals which might enable him to approach in safety the sacred places of another people. In later times, white settlers were unwittingly to cause much misery to native peoples by pushing them back into foreign territories beset with dangers unknown, and no less real for being spiritual.

But within his own territory, the native was protected in more ways than one. Here he was most intimately at home. From earliest childhood, he grew in knowledge of its resources of food and water and, wandering over it, he came to know all its natural features.

These were not mere physical variations of the earth's surface; they were the scene and product of his ancestral history. So he was bound to his territory in a spiritual relation that grew closer and richer as he grew in knowledge of tribal lore. Much of this knowledge he acquired in childhood by hearing those legends and watching those dances to which there was no reserve of secrecy. Much more he learned from the time he was 'made man', when, step by step, the more secret cult of his people was made known to him, and he himself was entrusted with its preservation and its passing on. So at all stages his territory was being peopled for him by his ancestors, whose deeds might belong to the remote 'dream-time', but who were nevertheless the enduring progenitors of himself and his fellows.

If the present, the remote past, and the clan or tribal territory were fused together in this fashion, the aboriginal had a yet closer relation with nature. This arose from the totemic associations with natural species and natural phenomena that attached to his birth and to the various tribal divisions to which he belonged—clan and moiety, section and sub-section. In some cases the totem was little more than an emblem, a mode of distinguishing the different groups; but in others it approached a personal identity between the native and the plant or animal of his totem.

So may be realized his love of home. He knew the land and all the species that grew and lived on it; he knew, in greater or less degree, its legendary history and its spiritual inhabitants; and, in the sense that he and his fellows were identical with their ancestors, it was their own creation. To leave it was to venture into the fearful unknown; but within it he dealt with familiar spirits. Even in the legends, this feeling for the tribal territory appears, and modern anthropologists have remarked on its strength among the living aborigines.

Dr Strehlow translates an Aranda native's comment on a deserted soak in the dry country of central Australia:

There is little here for strangers to see; there is no mountain cave here, only a storehouse in a mulga tree. But though the soak has been forsaken by almost all our people, a few of us old men still care for it. It still holds me fast; and I shall tend it while I can; while I live, I shall love to gaze on this ancient soil.

The primitive culture of the Australian aborigines was not a simple culture. The primitiveness of weapons and of the material mode of life stands in contrast with the intricacy and elaboration of social organization, cults and languages. The reader is referred to the anthropological works named in the bibliography for discussion of the subtleties of the kinship system and the division of tribes into clans and moieties, sections, sub-sections, and semi-moieties. Here only the most generalized account can be given of those features of tribal custom and government which seem to have been fairly common through all the great variations from tribe to tribe and region to region.

Tradition, the rule of the elders, the secret cults and attachment to tribal or clan territory made for social cohesion. In one respect, aboriginal culture as a whole presents a picture of social fragmentation; for the tribes, or, in such regions as East Arnhem Land where tribal organization is either weak or non-existent, the *hordes*, had little regular intercourse other than recurrent meetings for common ceremonies or for hospitalities. But within the tribal or other group, the society was very tightly knit under the rule of tradition interpreted by the older men. If this checked initiative, it gave a sense of belonging, of knowing one's place, of security; and that sense was strengthened by the white magic of traditional ceremonial.

But there was black magic as well as white, and all was not

security. In those areas where death was thought of as always due to personal malignancy, the search for the person responsible was the beginning of a chain of violence. And the secret cults contained such sorcery as bone-pointing, from which an aboriginal surely died, unless his tribal medicine man were able to protect him by still stronger magic. It was the important role of the medicine men— Professor Elkin's 'aboriginal men of high degree'—that, by all their methods of suggestion and secret magic, they protected the aboriginal from the undermining fears that could attack him. Even so, the stability and security of aboriginal life had its obverse of brutality and fear. So, too, in much tribal lore, the picture of a past golden age in which lands now arid flowed with water and teemed with game is balanced by tales of violence and treachery on a scale unmatched in later tribal experience.

But all in all, before European settlement, the aborigines had attained a successful relation with the land, living from it without destroying either the land or the delicate balance of the various forms of nature in it. So they lived, islanded for centuries on the margins of space, unknowing as Europe's ships edged their way around the Cape and across the Indian Ocean, around the Horn and across the Pacific, converging landfall by landfall towards the rich markets of the East.

3

THE FOUNDATION OF AN EMPIRE

Captain James Cook's exploration of the eastern coast of Australia in 1770 was made almost 300 years after Vasco da Gama's discovery of the sea route to India; for the westerlies, which favoured the rapid discovery of Australia from the west, long delayed its discovery from the east. Cook's great voyage might seem a splendid prelude to British settlement in the South Seas; but it was not thoughts of empire which followed discovery with settlement, but the irksome problem of the disposal of Britain's numerous convicts.

At least, such is the traditional view of Australian historians. In 1952 it was challenged in a paper read to historians in Hobart by Mr K. M. Dallas who argued that Botany Bay was chosen to provide a maritime base to support British trade with China, the Americas and the Pacific. So thoughts of empire were brought back into the story. The East India Company's hostility to any intrusion in that area, over the British trade of which it held a monopoly, and some disillusionment with colonies of settlement after the American Revolution, discouraged talk of settlement, but there was no end to advocacy of naval and trading posts in the Southern Pacific, an advocacy obviously known to the makers of British policy. So Mr Dallas's argument was feasible, but failed to gain acceptance because no documentary evidence could be found to establish that the British Government did indeed choose Botany Bay for these reasons.

In 1966 in his *Tyranny of Distance* Professor Geoffrey Blainey looked at Mr Dallas's argument once more in an attempt to solve the riddle: 'why did Britain send its convicts to a country which was so remote that it thrust as many disadvantages on the English taxpayer as on the convicts themselves?' In view of the relative nearness of the American colonies, previously used as a dumping place for convicts and of the other places considered as an alternative, he rejected the traditional argument that Botany Bay was chosen because its very remoteness gave ex-convicts little hope of returning to trouble their mother country. He found the solution to the riddle in the reference in Lord Sydney's 'Heads of a Plan' of 1786 to the valuable naval stores—flax for sailcloth and cables, timber for masts and spars—to be hoped for from the settlement and in the instruction to Governor Phillip to settle Norfolk Island where both the flax and the tall Norfolk pines grew. In these references Professor Blainey found the solution to the riddle.

In short, while not rejecting Dallas's feasible but unproven reference to the trades in tea, furs, whales and Spanish loot, Blainey concluded, 'Much evidence, hitherto hidden or discarded, suggests that Australia was first settled with the twin hopes of giving England the naval supplies it needed and ridding England of the people it didn't need.'

The controversy continues, but it would be certainly unwise to omit naval and mercantilist thoughts as irrelevant to a colonising venture undertaken by the greatest naval and trading power of the time.

But would the settlement of Botany Bay have been undertaken for these reasons alone? The problem of finding a new home for American loyalists after the American revolution did not spur indolent governments into this action although Botany Bay was twice proposed for this purpose.

On the other hand, no blind eye could for long be turned on the spread of crime and the increasing number of convicts who could no longer be decanted into the American colonies. The increase of population in the British Isles, beginning its acceleration in the later years of the century, and the revolutions in agriculture and industry, were to make Britain a wealthy and powerful country. But they did so at the cost of a vast upheaval in British society.

Only the early beginnings of the economic revolution can be seen in the eighteenth century; yet even these beginnings, together with the long years of war and the crowding years of famine and high prices in the latter half of the century, brought insecurity and want to many people They were being uprooted in numerous villages, crowded into the tenements and infested alleys of the towns, hit by rising prices, and deprived of the stability of long custom and the incentive of secure employment. They were ready material for schooling in crime. But the effects of criminality were more obvious than its causes. 'They starve and freeze and rot among themselves,' Fielding had written, 'but they beg and steal and rob among their betters.'

Lacking an efficient police, the orderly sections of the eighteenth-century society felt themselves to be defenceless before spreading crime, and sought defence in an increasing savagery of the criminal law. As penalties were increased without system, the law grew chaotic as well as savage. Neither savagery nor chaos lessened the habitual criminal's readiness to gamble on his chance, and pickpockets plied their trade in the crowds that watched pickpockets being hanged at Tyburn. Meanwhile, the social upheaval continued which nurtured into crime many who in more favourable conditions might well have lived orderly and decent lives.

So the number of convicted persons continued to rise, particularly in the more depressed areas of southern England and Ireland; and the former outlet by way of transportation to the American colonies was closed. When the gaols were crowded, hulks were pressed into service, to become crowded in their turn.

This was the situation which pressed Lord Sydney into the action which founded Australia; but Professor Blainey may be correct in supposing that a cheaper solution would have been found if the disposal of convicts had been the only object. Nevertheless, one may doubt whether Lord Sydney and his advisers had any precise conception of the disadvantages which the choice of Botany Bay might bring to the English taxpayer.

That choice was made in 1786 when it was decided to send 750 convicts to establish a penal settlement on the shores of Botany Bay, a place which Sir Joseph Banks had recommended for this purpose some seven years earlier.

Whether or not the Government looked much beyond the solution of a present inconvenience, there was a vision of the future in the Government's official representative, Captain Arthur Phillip, R.N., who did not doubt a greater future even in the grim infancy of a penal colony. Cast in a mould of quiet, understated, industrious heroism—and how common this was in his service—Phillip grew with the responsibilities of his task, and displayed behind the prose of official decorum, the poetry of the visionary. But if he dared to dream of the future of the community whose miserable birth he was attending, he did not desert the disciplined practicality of his training, and he laid, by industrious attention to detail, the only possible foundations from which those dreams might grow.

On 26 January 1788, Phillip moored his transports, carrying almost 1,500 people, in Sydney Cove. Not for the last time occurred a recurrent motif of Australian settlement—the dumping of large numbers of people in scarce-known territories without preliminary survey. The birth of this newest of British colonies was celebrated

B

with toasts and volleys of musketry, and the flag was unfurled at the head of the cove where none but aborigines had trodden before.

Phillip, whose quietness, like still waters, ran deep, saw this as the moment of 'the foundation of an empire'. How little there was to support his belief! 'It is a shameful and unblessed thing', Bacon had written in the earliest days of English colonization, 'to take the scum of people, and wicked condemned men, to be the people with whom you plant'; and Phillip's repeated appeals to the Government to send out free settlers echoed this view. In fact, the first fleet had been welcomed as a heaven-sent opportunity to clear the gaols of the aged, diseased and mentally disordered. Phillip's task of colonizing with such wretched material was not made easier, at the end of a long supply line, by the shortage and uncertainty of supplies, or by the failure of the Government to reply to his requests for skilled farmers and adequate farming implements.

His task was made still more difficult by the refusal of the officers of the garrison to have any part in the control of convicts, and most of all by the sustained spleen of his lieutenant-governor, Major Ross, Commandant of Marines, who wrote in a characteristic outburst:

I do not scruple to pronounce that in the whole world there is not a worse country than what we have yet seen of this. All that is contiguous to us is so very barren and forbidding that it may with truth be said here nature is reversed, and if not so, she is nearly worn out, for almost all the seeds we have put into the ground has rotted, and have no doubt but will, like the wood of this vile country when burned or rotten, turn to sand.

For there was no escaping the fact that New South Wales was founded as a gaol, and this first phase in the changing pattern of settlement persisted for a long time. Convicts continued to be sent to New South Wales until 1840, and to Tasmania until 1852, while Western Australia, languishing for want of labour, asked for and received convicts from 1850 to 1868. In the first fifty years, at least, no Australian question could be considered without reference to the convict system.

But the very word 'system' is misleading, for the striking feature of it is the haphazardness of its devising and the uncertainty of its administration. Not until transportation to New South Wales had ceased was a complete system of convict discipline devised by the authorities at home. It is true that there had been earlier attempts to bring uniformity into the variety of practices that had grown up in the penal colonies; but it is an example of the uncertainties of the situation that as late as 1827 Chief Justice Forbes of New South

Wales could throw doubt on the legal validity of tickets of leave which governors from Phillip onwards had granted without question of their right to do so.

In fact, what had happened was that when New South Wales was founded much earlier practices were continued with an adjustment so sketchy as to underline the general planlessness with which Pitt's Government founded its new colony. Before their revolt, the American colonies had received convicts from Great Britain at the rate of about 1,000 a year. In those days, a property in the services of the convict had been assigned to the shipping contractors whose profit came from the sale—or subassignment—of those services to the colonists for the term of the convict's sentence. With the establishment of the penal colony in New South Wales, convicts were assigned on arrival in the colony to the person of the governor, who, with little qualification, was left free to reassign their services to settlers or to retain them on government works.

The governor was also allowed to emancipate convicts for good conduct; and in the course of time, conventions developed by which a convict could pass through progressive steps from servitude to liberty, receiving a ticket of leave, a conditional pardon and even an absolute pardon before the expiry of his term of sentence.

The plans devised by the governors did not escape criticism, particularly if they appeared to run counter to the constant pressure for economy which colonial secretaries, themselves dogged by the lords of the treasury, passed on to the governors. 'I have only to assure you', wrote Earl Bathurst to Governor Macquarie—it is true in a time of financial stringency, but the theme recurs at all times—'that you cannot give yourself a stronger Claim to the Approbation of His Majesty's Government, than by proving, from the Retrenchments made by you on the present occasion, the sincerity of your desire to adopt, as the Rule of your government, a System of regular and rigid Economy.'

In all, from first to last, about 160,000 persons arrived in Australia as convicts, and the greatest number of these arrived between 1815 and 1852. Until the ending of transportation to New South Wales and the establishment of the probation system, the great majority of convicts were assigned by the governors to the private service of settlers, particularly when settlement was spreading after 1815. Assignment had the advantage that it cost less than the retention of convicts in government stations, and that, as settlers grew in number, it provided them with cheap if unwilling labour. Further, it must be said that the worst evils of the convict days affected, not the great majority assigned to settlers, but the minority in barracks, road gangs and, worst of all, the penal settlements, particularly those of Norfolk Island and Port Arthur.

Nevertheless, assignment suffered from grave disadvantages. In the days when penal science, from Beccaria to Bentham, pinned its faith on certainty as the essence of punishment, the essence of assignment was its uncertainty. It was correctly described as 'a lottery', 'the greatest and worst of all lotteries', in which punishment was in no way correlated with the nature or gravity of the crime. Lord John Russell declared that 'a man is estimated by his capacity as a colonist; not by his crime as a felon'. A House of Commons Committee of 1837–8 (the Molesworth Committee) came to the same conclusion; 'the previous occupation of a convict in this country', it reported, 'mainly determines his condition in the penal colonies' 'Mechanics', being scarce, fared best.

'Convicts who are mechanics,' reported the Molesworth Committee, 'are as well, if not better treated, than those, who are domestic servants; for as every kind of skilled labour is very scarce in New South Wales, a convict, who has been a blacksmith, carpenter, mason, cooper, wheelwright, or gardener, is a most valuable servant, worth three or four ordinary convicts; he is eagerly sought after, and great interest is made to obtain him. As a mechanic can scarcely be compelled by punishment to exert his skill, it is for the interest of the master to conciliate his convict mechanic in order to induce him to work well; in too many cases this is effected by granting to the skilled convict various indulgences; by paying him wages; by allotting to him task work, and by permitting him, after the performance of the task, to work on his own account; and lastly, by conniving at, or overlooking disorderly conduct; for the most skilful mechanics are generally the worst behaved, and most drunken.'

Both Russell and the committee, however, exaggerated the degree of regularity with which a convict's usefulness determined his punishment. It was very much more a matter of chance whether he were retained in government service or assigned to a private settler, and if the latter, whether he were assigned to an easy or a harsh master. He might be fortunate enough to be assigned to the Macarthurs of Camden who got fair service by easy rule; he might, however, be one of the unfortunates assigned to James Mudie, author of *The Felonry of New South Wales*, at his preposterous Castle Forbes. The rule of terror at this place became so notorious that Governor Bourke removed Mudie from the Commission of the Peace. Mudie admitted later to the Select Committee of Transportation of 1837 that he left New South Wales because he 'was compelled to quit'. He considered himself 'perfectly unsafe to remain' after being removed from the Commission of the Peace.

Between these extremes there was every degree of variation; but in general the sanction which enforced the obedience of assigned servants was the lash, tempered in some cases by bribery. In certain respects, they were not slaves. Their terms of servitude were limited; they could not be bought and sold; and their children were born free. But there were many elements of slavery in their lot.

They could not be flogged except by the order of a magistrate other than the person to whom they were assigned. But as the magistrate was in almost all cases a fellow landholder and employer of convicts, the word of the master weighed more than that of an accused convict. Therry comments on the difficulty experienced in finding suitable magistrates for the Commission of the Peace; and it was Lord John Russell who commented that in no other part of the British Empire did magistrates possess powers so great or so capable of abuse.

Despite attempts to check abuse and to give the convict some right to complain, the lash was never still, brutalizing both the convict and his master. Absence from work, or refusal to work, drunken and disorderly conduct, frivolous complaints and 'insolence' were the common grounds of punishment, and insolence might consist in looks as well as in words. And, indeed, there was plain contradiction between the common interest of masters in gaining profit from convict labour and the common interest of convicts in avoiding as much as possible of that labour which was for them nothing but punishment.

The behaviour of assigned convicts was generally reported 'good' in the sense that they did not turn in violence against their masters, except in isolated cases as at Castle Forbes where exceptional brutality drove them beyond endurance. But the evidence before committees of inquiry suggests a general reign of petty terror, as masters, who feared their convict servants or knew of no other incentive to work, held over them the fear of the lash. There were many methods of inspiring fear. One newly arrived convict was taken by his master to watch hangings and warned to learn his lesson. A man due for a ticket of leave or a conditional pardon might have his hopes disappointed if his master reported adversely of him.

All, indeed, was caprice. And yet this very capriciousness gave assignment one of its advantages over the other forms of punishment then in use in the colonies. Every variety could be found in the housing, clothing and feeding of the assigned convict. Control ranged from brutal severity to indifference. The work to which he might be put varied from clearing scrub and tending sheep to acting as tutor to his master's children. His emancipation might be fast or slow. There was no equal justice, no tempering of punishment to crime. It was in fact a lottery.

But it was a lottery in which there were prizes. There were chinks in the armour of that rule of terror which in the penal thought of the time was expected at once to punish, deter and reform. The assigned servant often knew the degradation and misery of the slave; but he might be in no worse case than an indentured servant. Indeed, he might be, as to food, in better case than the free rural labourer in England; and if assignment rarely encouraged reform, it did not always prevent it.

The great majority of convicts were assigned for all or part of their terms of servitude. A minority were retained under direct government control. Some of these were in no very different condition from that of assigned servants, working as clerks and messengers for official departments. But for the greater part, they were herded together in barracks, road and building gangs, chain gangs, and in the penal settlements such as Norfolk Island and Port Arthur. These last, the source of the most notorious stories of the convict days, were mainly places of secondary punishment for offences committed after arrival in the colony.

All contemporary evidence is clear that the lot of the convicts in the gangs and still more in the settlements was far more terrible than that of the assigned servants. Here there were no prizes. The caprice which allowed contradictory touches of humanity to break into assignment was absent. Life conformed more to a pattern, and it was a pattern of gloom and depravity.

Assignment diffused the convicts throughout the free population and allowed thereby a degree of normality into their lives. 'It was the punishment', Sir John Franklin told his council when assignment had already been condemned by the Molesworth Committee, 'in which the state of the convict is the least removed from the natural condition. It is the least artificial of all punishments.'

But the convicts of barracks and gangs and penal settlements were cut off from the community at large, neither to pollute it nor to be further polluted by it. And, to the degree that they were isolated from the free community, they were thrown together in the abnormal society of the unfree, with no separation of petty from grave offender, so that the young in crime 'learned the deeper mysteries of the masonry of crime' from those more advanced. In such company, it was the graduates of higher degree who established the conventions of depravity to which all must conform. The end was degradation for all. Survival required the suppression of all disabling sensitiveness, of all humanity, of all moral conscience. The weak must learn to defend themselves against the strong by deceit and sycophancy. In a stark struggle for existence, the strong had every incentive to trample the weak. Worst feature of all in these artificial communities was the prevalence of unnatural crime. The reports make sad and sordid reading.

These things reached their worst in the penal settlements, and, as Governor Arthur reported, 'they grew weary of life'. Dr Ullathorne, a Catholic priest who visited Norfolk Island after a mutiny there in 1834, gave the following evidence to a select committee of the horror of that place:

I said a few words to induce them to resignation, and I then stated the names of those who were to die; and it is a remarkable fact, that as I mentioned the names of those men who were to die, they one after the other, as their names were pronounced, dropped on their knees and thanked God that they were to be delivered from that horrible place, whilst the others remained standing mute; it was the most horrible scene I ever witnessed.

Women convicts were either assigned to settlers or put to work in barracks, the 'female factories'. Their corruption had generally gone far before they arrived. Assignment was sometimes the road to marriage, but all too often to prostitution. The female factories were still more reliable schools of vice. Unable to use the lash, no supervision succeeded in maintaining discipline over them, and despite the efforts of some good people, the task was for the most part abandoned as hopeless.

Humanitarians and systematic colonizers grew restive during the 'thirties at the disturbing reports of transportation that reached the mother country. In 1837, a select committee under Sir William Molesworth inquired into the subject. This committee represented the party of systematic colonizers, who looked to revenue from land sales to finance the immigration of free labourers. Their condemnation of the assignment system was certain.

It is hard to resist Archbishop Whateley's comment on the report of this committee. 'The one part—the main part of the report', he declared, 'seems to spring naturally out of the evidence like a tree growing from its own roots; the other part looks like a graft, with totally different foliage and fruit, brought from elsewhere and inserted into the stock.' Evidence of the abuses of assignment coincided with theory and supported the recommendation that 'transportation to New South Wales and to the settled districts of Van Diemen's Land, should be discontinued as soon as practicable'. In keeping with this recommendation, transportation to New South Wales was ended in 1840.

But the evidence heard by the committee had made it clear that the evils of assignment were as virtues beside those of the penal settlements. Yet the committee, while urging the ending of assignment, also recommended the establishment in Norfolk Island and on Tasman's Pensinula of penal settlements for long-term prisoners isolated from the free community. It is true that the committee had in mind penal settlements of a very different nature from those which had earlier brought horror to the fair shores of Norfolk Island and Port Arthur.

They were much influenced by Alexander Maconochie, who believed that the worst feature of the old system was the uncertainty and the favouritism attending remission of sentence. This, he argued, should be gained as a reward of good conduct and good work, according to a fixed and known scale of marks. It is fair to say that Maconochie looked to hope rather than terror as the incentive to reform; and his system provided for a relaxation of discipline, for useful training, as the convict passed from the initial stage of solitary confinement to the later stages of punishment.

In Maconochie's ideas and in those of the Molesworth Committee there was humanity and a good deal of wisdom. But there was a fatal lack of realism. The Government allowed Maconochie to try out his ideas from 1840 to 1844 in a new penal settlement on Norfolk Island; and it is clear that he achieved some success, even with men who had seemed beyond reformation. But any full trial of his ideas would have required an expenditure of public money on the accommodation and training of convicts and on the employment of a superior type of overseer which, as all past experience made clear, would not be allowed. It is difficult to resist the conclusion that it was the cost of his system which brought about his removal from office in 1844.

In Tasmania, a second experiment was tried in the form of the probation system, fully established in 1842 after some tentative beginnings. After two years in probation gangs a prisoner might for good conduct receive a probation-pass allowing him to work for wages, while further good conduct would be rewarded by a ticket of leave.

The probation system was a disastrous failure. The evils of the old gangs and settlements were reproduced in the 'probation gangs'. Moreover, there was no hope that the small island of Tasmania could employ the whole stream of convict migration, now diverted to it from the mainland, even if it had escaped the depression of the early 'forties. There was, in fact, no ready labour market to absorb and perhaps reform the products of probation. There was widespread unemployment among the pass-holders and the stringent economies of depression years made it difficult for the Government to keep even the gangs employed.

Rumours that reached England persuaded Gladstone in 1846 to order Superintendent La Trobe of Port Phillip to cross Bass Strait and report on the system. La Trobe's fair and well-informed report declared that it had been 'a fatal experiment as far as it has proceeded, and the sooner it is put an end to, the better for the credit of the nation and of humanity'. This advice was taken, and the later administration of convict discipline in Tasmania escaped at least the worst evils of earlier days.

But how often has the essence of this experience been reproduced in our history! As colonies in the making, we invited the attention of the experimenter and theorist who too often assumed a perfection in both governments and citizens which can never safely be assumed. Uncomfortable experience of the results of the theories of the 'systematic' colonizers bred in the colonies a distrust of theory which was probably carried too far; for it might be argued that the fault was not in theorizing, but in theorizing badly, by leaving out of account such important facts as the normal fallibility of human beings.

Transportation of convicts to Western Australia, coming later, could benefit by old experience. The convicts were more carefully selected, and a system was worked out which combined the benefits of the old assignment system with an avoidance of its uncertainty. Selected from prisoners of good behaviour in English prisons, convicts were first sent to a prison in Fremantle known to them as 'the College'. During this stage of public detention, they were employed on public works in and around Fremantle.

They were then released on a restricted ticket of leave and sent out in parties for work on roads and public buildings. These parties were not isolated from the free community and were allowed considerable liberty. It was, in fact, a stage during which the convict had many opportunities to learn something of his new home and of the types of employment it might eventually offer him. The main sanction of discipline at this stage was the knowledge that misconduct would revoke his probationary ticket of leave and postpone his conditional pardon.

The next stage was a full ticket of leave which enabled the convict, under certain restriction of movement and behaviour, to earn wages and acquire property. From this stage, he graduated to a conditional pardon which left on him only the restriction that he could not return to Great Britain, nor go to Victoria and South Australia, until the whole term of his sentence had expired.

Western Australia did not escape entirely from the disorders that everywhere accompanied transportation; but it did escape the worst evils of that system, and a languishing colony was put on its feet at a difficult time by an influx of labour that proved to be moderately willing and efficient.

There has from time to time been much discussion of the influence of convicts on our history. Anxiety to disprove any suggestion of an enduring taint has made for emphasis on the savagery of the penal code and the supposed predominance of trivial offenders. But the great majority of convicts were sent out when the penal code was already being reformed. The noble poachers and political martyrs of patriotic imagination provided a tiny minority and most of the convicts were thieves and pickpockets, boys and young men for the most part, from the alleys and courts of urban slums.

Anxiety to believe otherwise betrays a readiness to suppose that conviction of crime implied a biologically transmissible disposition to offend against the law. There is no ground for such a belief, and no reason, in view of the many other factors then making for crime, to suppose that any abnormal proportion of the convicts was of particularly low intelligence. Environment had much more than parentage to do with the moulding of the native sons, and, in so far as that environment offered greater hope than the convicts had found at home, it fostered a community that grew less vicious as the corrupting effects of penal discipline became a bad memory of the past. It was frequently a matter for comment that the native-born, the currency lads and lasses, were better than their convict parents.

Even Commissioner Bigge, who was not given to praise of the less respectable orders of society, echoed this impression in a rather quaint description:

The class of inhabitants that have been born in the colony affords a remarkable exception to the moral and physical character of their parents: they are generally tall in person, and slender in their limbs, of fair complexion, and small features. They are capable of undergoing more fatigue, and are less exhausted by labour than native Europeans; they are active in their habits, but remarkably awkward in their movements. In their tempers they are quick and irascible, but not vindictive; and I only repeat the testimony of persons who have had many opportunities of observing them, that they neither inherit the vices nor the feelings of their parents.

The enduring effects of Australia's convict stage are probably small and at that intangible. Professor Russel Ward in *The Australian*

Legend has ascribed to our convict origins an enduring disrespect for authority, and the hold of 'mateship' on later Australian working-class history.[1] A persistent sensitiveness to criticism may also owe something to awareness of the convict element in Australian history; but this may just as well be the result of our closeness to the stage of colonization, bond or free.

The fact remains that the convict system dominated the first fifty years of Australian history. There is no evidence that it succeeded in deterring potential criminals at home; despite all its misery, the reports of those to whom it had brought unexpected opportunity created the legend of the jingle:

> Let us haste away to Botany Bay
> Where there is plenty and nothing to pay.

If it failed to deter, its chance successes in the work of reformation were at least balanced by the efficiency of its penal gangs and settlements in the work of corruption. As a penalty, it long suffered from its uncertainty, the lack of any regular relation between the gravity of the offence and the degree of suffering imposed on the convict. While it lasted, it besotted and brutalized the penal colonies of eastern Australia, and made for a class consciousness which might have been more serious had not the wide diffusion of opportunity in growing colonies blunted its edge.

Nevertheless, the convict system played a constructive role in the history of this country. It provided the motive for settlement and a supply of labour for its early development. That labour may have been unwilling and, often enough, shiftless and inefficient. But it was the convicts who built the roads and bridges and government buildings of the infant colonies. It was they who built and served the private homes and wharves and warehouses of early Sydney and Hobart Town. It was they, even when free immigrants were coming in plenty, who tended the flocks that gave the colonies their staple and changed the attitude of both investors and governments at home.

The cheapness of their labour, as some of the settlers claimed in a protest against the ending of transportation to New South Wales, attracted both capital and moneyed immigrants to the colonies. It was this very cheapness that moved other less wealthy immigrants, who arrived in large numbers in the 'thirties and 'forties, to welcome the ending of transportation and to fight later attempts to renew it. By that time, its day was past; but, forced and inefficient though it was, it had laid in wretchedness the foundations of the later free colonies for which no other labour could then have been secured.

[1] See p. 153–6 below.

4

FROM GAOL TO COLONY

Convicts were transported to one part or another of Australia over a long period of eighty years. Nevertheless, it was clear from the outset that New South Wales and its off-shoots could not remain merely 'an extensive gaol to the empire'.

There was no thought of taking the convicts back to an unwelcoming mother country, and they became free in time either by expiry or by remission of their sentences. So there grew up in the penal colonies, side by side with those who were still convicts, the community of those who had become 'free by servitude'. Once even partially free, they went about the ordinary business of free men.

A minority rose to wealth and influence as merchants, publicans and professional men, and a few of them in the squatting age as pastoralists. The majority formed classes of free labourers and shepherds, artisans, shopkeepers, and farmers. From them, too, came those earlier 'squatters' of ill-repute, the keepers of grog-shanties who stole the sheep of their respectable neighbours and, through the supply of rum, preyed on the wages of their workmen. Whatever they became, once free, society grew more complex, and the task of administering a gaol was vastly complicated by the problem of governing the growing numbers of those who had graduated into freedom.

Nor, indeed, had it ever been supposed that New South Wales should be a Devil's Island receiving only convicts. Governor Phillip's instructions showed a disposition to encourage any free settlers who might offer to go, and he did not cease to ask for them. None arrived in his time, nor until 1795; and their number remained small during the years of war until 1815. They were, with few exceptions, poor stuff. Of more than 150 families, declared Surgeon Thomson in 1804, he knew 'very few indeed between whom and the convict he could

draw the smallest discrimination. . . . Some have been people of very
suspicious characters, and have narrowly escaped being sent out
against their inclinations; others, low mechanics who have failed in
business, with long families, who had they remained in England,
would have become burdensome to their parishes; others, men of
dissolute and drunken habits'. That opinion is strongly supported by
other evidence.

The number of these free settlers who had always been free was
supplemented by soldiers of the garrison who chose to stay in the
colony. They were placed on small holdings, but proved for the most
part complete failures as farmers; having lived idle and useless lives,
declared one report, they were unfitted for hard labour.

Not until the proven promise of Australian Merinos made the long
journey to the under parts of the earth seem worth while did the
free immigration of men of capital grow into more than a tiny
trickle; and not until schemes of assisted immigration carried the
surplus poor of the parishes to the colonies in the 1830s and 1840s,
did the number of free labouring immigrants vie with the number of
convicts. But from the first instruction to Phillip to give encouragement to any free settlers who might care to go to New South Wales,
the potential threat to the penal purposes of colonization was present.

There were other straws in the wind which pointed in the same
direction. The arguments of strategic and commercial advantage
which had been used by the proposers of a settlement of American
loyalists in New South Wales were to some degree incorporated in
the foundation of the penal colony. The governor was commanded
to occupy Norfolk Island 'as a spot which may hereafter become
useful' and to 'prevent it being occupied by the subjects of any other
European power'. He was to attend to the cultivation of flax, not
only for clothing, 'but from its superior excellence for a variety of
maritime purposes', and he was to reserve to the Crown timber
which might be fit for naval use. The time might come, in short,
when Botany Bay might have other uses than as a receptacle for the
unwanted criminal classes.

The same possibility was underlined in the early years of the nineteenth century by the precautionary colonization of other parts of
Australia in order to prevent any French claim to that area. For this
reason, when Baudin's exploring expedition aroused suspicion,
settlements were founded in Van Diemen's Land in 1803–4 and a
short-lived settlement in Port Phillip. So began the colony of Van
Diemen's Land, later called Tasmania, which remained technically
part of New South Wales until 1825.

None of this amounted to active and purposeful colonization, and penal purposes remained dominant. Nevertheless, strategic and commercial afterthoughts pointed to the possibility that the Australian settlements might come in time to play a different and more dignified role in the imperial scheme.

In time, but not yet. The first pattern of settlement in Australia was simply the painful effort of a convict community, banished to a difficult environment at the end of a long and precarious supply line, to feed itself. The difficulties of strange country and of poor and inadequate equipment—there was no plough in the colony during its first few years—were multiplied by the fact that the only labour available was the unwilling labour of convicts.

'If fifty farmers were sent out with their families', wrote Phillip, 'they would do more in a year in rendering this colony independent of the mother country, as to provisions, than a thousand convicts.' Having no free settlers, he was compelled, much against his desire, to rely in the main on public farms, their surface scratched by convicts whose unwillingness of spirit was supported, in the starvation time, by a real weakness of the flesh. For the failure of food-ships to arrive reduced all, from governor to convicts, to strict and inadequate rations for a large part of Phillip's governorship.

As time went on, Phillip tried to grow more food by placing emancipists—convicts whose sentences had been remitted or expired —and some soldiers as settlers on small holdings. This was for him not only an economic measure, but a means towards the redemption of convicts as decent citizens. For he matched the severity with which he punished breaches of discipline with a belief that transportation could best serve the end of reforming the convict by holding out hope and encouragement. When he left the colony in 1792, close on two-thirds of the cultivated land still formed the government farms; but more than one-third was being farmed by small settlers, and this proportion was increasing.

It might seem that the cultivation of small holdings was coming to be the main pattern of settlement in New South Wales. There was no possibility that it could continue to be so.

Phillip himself had sought permission to grant larger holdings to officers of the garrison. Between his departure and the arrival in 1795 of Captain John Hunter, his successor as governor, there was an interval of almost three years during which the colony was ruled by the officers of the garrison, the New South Wales Corps. These officers used their position without scruple to acquire fortunes and estates, and thereby hastened the growth of a capitalist economy in New South Wales. But they did not create something which would not have developed without them, although it might have developed more slowly and with less injustice. There were both physical and historical reasons why the pattern of small holdings could not be indefinitely continued, and why the economic and social life of the colony should come to be dominated by wealthy landowners and merchants employing labour.

Both soil and climate were adverse to the small settler. True peasant farming is scarcely possible in Australia, and commercial farming required either larger holdings than the usual grants to emancipists and small settlers, or preliminary works of development which could come only late in the history of the colonies. Successful wheat-farming, for example, needed much larger holdings than were customary, and the expenditure of much more capital than the small settlers of this time could command. Their lack of capital and the smallness of their holdings condemned the majority of them to a hopeless struggle with debt, from which only the few could escape who could develop market gardening close to the infant townships.

The coastal lands near Sydney were for the most part unsuitable for wheat. Apart from the unpredictable but recurrent devastations of both floods and drought, there were early complaints of smut in the wheat, and, given unskilled management and lack of capital, of declining yields. The good wheat lands of New South Wales lie inland of the Dividing Range. Their use for farming depended on a number of conditions which could not then exist—on cheap transport which came only with the railway, on expensive schemes of water conservation, on the breeding of drought and rust-resisting wheats, and on the application of study and money to supply the deficiencies of Australian soils.

Production of crops requiring smaller areas than wheat had for the most part to await expensive public schemes of irrigation and marketing which also could come only late in the history of Australia, and then only in limited areas. So, too, dairying on small holdings was limited by the size of the population until the rise of refrigeration late in the nineteenth century offered a larger market overseas. In short, closer settlement was bound to be a late phase in Australian history, and, in the early years, it could not develop far beyond a limited amount of market gardening and a struggling, inefficient attempt to produce for the commissariat market.

If for such reasons small settlers could not be typical of Australian colonization, there were also historical reasons for the early rise of an economy directed by men of capital. The Australian colonies were established, for whatever dubious purposes, by the greatest trading nation of the world at that time; and it was certain that sooner or later Englishmen, imbued with the spirit of the *entrepreneur*, the dominant spirit of their age and country, would seek openings for their enterprise in these new parts. The great migration of English capital overseas was not to begin until after the wars, for savings were absorbed in loans to the national debt and their expansion was checked by wartime taxation. But the commercial enterprise of a nation of shopkeepers penetrated the seven seas well in advance of absentee investment.

Consider the example of Robert Campbell, merchant of Calcutta, who came to Sydney in 1798 to set up a branch of his firm in the new colony. His activities ranged from trading, the seal fisheries and banking to the development of landed estates. Sydney became his home and not a passing place of business, and he ended his career as its wealthiest merchant and as a pastoral pioneer of the Canberra district. Consider also such ventures as those of the English firm of the Enderbys which was using Port Jackson as early as 1792 as a base for its ventures in the seal fisheries. The English settlements in New South Wales, it was clear, would not escape the restless probing for profitable opportunities which marked that expansive capitalist society.

This may enable us to see the rule of the New South Wales Corps in perspective. It had been formed for service in the remote colony in 1789. During the three years of their unrestricted rule its officers together with some civilian officials used their position and resources to build up a system of mutual favouritism and of monopolistic trading which all the efforts of Governors Hunter, King and Bligh in later years could not wholly break. Only when their final excess, the levying of a military rebellion against Governor Bligh in 1808, forced the government at home into slow and grudging action—for the Department of the Secretary of State for War, then responsible for colonies, had its hands full in coping with Bonaparte—was the corps disbanded and 'the Rum Ring' broken. The next governor, Lachlan Macquarie, arrived with his own regiment to support his rule.

The most profitable part of their monopolistic trading had been the import of rum, 'the ardent spirits of Bengal', and the colony was flooded with it. All the evils of Gin Lane were reproduced in the broken community which Phillip had tried to save by a combination of severity and nurture. No efforts of the governors could replace Gin Lane by Beer Street, for their orders could be enforced only by the men whose interest it was to flout them. The rum traffic, declared Governor Hunter in just indignation, 'an angel from heaven possessing the omniscient attribute of the Divine Being would not have been able as a single individual, to prevent'.

The social effect of the rule of 'the Rum Corps' was to leave more vicious than it might otherwise have been a community that was already morally weak. The reformatory aim of Phillip's policy could not survive the rule of monopoly and rum. Beset by debt and besotted with drink, many of his small settlers sold out or surrendered their holdings to the two classes of people who profited from the rum traffic—the officers and their friends of 'the Rum Ring', and their publican agents. Debt and rum paralysed the wills of those who did not sell out, and, if they did not create, at least encouraged the raffish carelessness evident in their manners and their dwellings and in the haphazard management of their farms.

The economic effects of the New South Wales Corps' monopoly, however, may be exaggerated. It had ruined many small settlers and hastened the accumulation of considerable estates and capital in the hands of a few people. It is true that the actual number of small-holders increased as sentences expired and settlers arrived; but they mattered far less in colonial farming at the end of the rule of the corps than the wealthy landowner using convict and ex-convict labour. But the profit-hunting activities of the corps did not bring in an element that would otherwise have been absent; they hastened but did not solely create the development of a capitalist economy in New South Wales.

The point has been obscured by the fact that John Macarthur, main architect of the monopoly, made his fortune in its dealings, and used it to demonstrate the possibilities of colonial fine wool. He had arrived in the colony as a lieutenant of the New South Wales Corps and resigned from it in 1801 to give his full attention to his private ventures.

The most quarrelsome subject in a quarrelsome community, his charm of manner and intelligence also made him the most able advocate of its dawning economic possibilities. He fought every governor from Hunter to Macquarie and yet returned from England, where he had been sent under arrest, with a large grant of crown land to carry on those experiments in the growing of fine wool with which he had impressed both manufacturers and officials at home. Rapacious and relentless in the pursuit of his advantage, he was at the same time a man of imagination who could resist the temptation of immediate gain in order to plan the greater result. So he was at once the brain and driving force of the monopoly and the prime discoverer of the colony's staple. He did more than any other single person by his work and his advocacy to change the attitude of British governments and British investors towards the penal colonies.

Yet when all is said, the rise of an economy directed by men of

capital was certain. For commercial enterprise was not confined to
the members of the rum ring. A few moneyed settlers were arriving
in the early years of the century, and some of the emancipists were
rising from small beginnings to affluence by the exercise of commercial shrewdness.

Let us look a little more widely at the search for profitable investment in the penal colonies. It was not at all evident in the early days
that wool was to supply the colonies with their staple commodity for
export. As late as 1819, Macarthur was complaining, with some
exaggeration, that his experiments in breeding sheep for wool were
stimulating neither interest nor imitation.

Flax, timber and coal were all tried. Flax was grown and used, but
on a small and fluctuating scale. Colonial timbers were plentifully
used for colonial purposes, for houses, furniture and small vessels;
and Australian cedar was exported to England for many years. But
less valuable timbers were a bulky expensive cargo to send round the
world, and the unfamiliar hardwoods created no demand that could
compete with the familiar timbers of nearer countries. One of the
first regular exports was coal from Newcastle on the Hunter River
north of Sydney. It provided a welcome lading for government
transports returning with empty holds and enabled the British
Government to supply its stations in India and at the Cape cheaply.
But it would be carrying coals to Newcastle to carry them to England,
and the Java market was more or less closed by the East India
Company's monopoly of trade in that region.

For a long time it seemed that sealing and whaling might provide
the infant colonies with their staple. Indeed, for some years, the
settlements of New South Wales and Van Diemen's Land, hemmed
between mountains and sea, were to all intents and purposes islands,
and it seemed that their destiny might lie out to sea rather than inland
over the mountains.

In 1804, Governor King reported that 'sealskins are the only
staple yet discovered here', and gave sealing as one of his objects in
settling Van Diemen's Land. Sealing, which began in the early 1790s,
was at its height at the turn of the century; but it rapidly declined as
the unrestrained slaughter both destroyed the source of supply and
depressed the market. A single brig brought 60,000 skins from the
South Antipodes in 1806, and cargoes of from 10,000 to 15,000 skins
were normal. It was a considerable trade while it lasted. In 1802,
Sydney merchants such as Robert Campbell, Kable and Underwood,
and the emancipist, Simeon Lord, were employing 200 men in sealing
gangs in Bass Strait.

To kill the seals, these men used aboriginal women who would

swim out to the seal rocks, lie down among the seals until their
suspicions were dulled, and then, at some concerted signal, rise and
club them to right and left. Often the seal meat was bartered to the
aborigines for kangaroo skins. By 1803, the sealers were moving
from the Straits to New Zealand and then south to Macquarie
Island, seeking new fields as the old were depleted. Their place in
the straits was taken by buccaneer gangs based on Kangaroo Island;
'a complete set of pirates' they were called. Indeed, the first settlement of South Australia was far less respectable than the official
settlement of thirty years later.

Whaling developed more slowly but lasted longer. Bay whalers
were the precursors of settlement in Victoria, South Australia,
Western Australia and New Zealand; and deep-sea whaling continued long after the decline of bay whaling. Even in 1860, thirty
whaling ships were sailing from Hobart as far as Kerguelen Island.
It was a valuable trade, and as late as 1833, the products of the whale
fishery made up half the exports of New South Wales. It was in the
following year that the picturesque Jorgen Jorgenson described
Hobart as 'enriched with oleaginous spoils'.

Sealing and whaling were only two aspects of colonial enterprise
that for a long time seemed to point to a maritime rather than a
landed development. In some neglect of the East India Company's
monopoly and of the navigation laws, colonial vessels traded far
and wide in the Pacific, as far afield as the coasts of Chile and north
to Batavia and China. The carriage of sandalwood and bêche-de-mer
from Fiji and the Marquesas Islands to China in return for tea was
the mainstay of this trade. It was ruined by the outrages committed
on the natives by the crews of colonial as of other vessels; and
for the colonials by the reassertion of the right of the East India
Company to monopolize such trade so far as it was in English
hands.

Nevertheless, the aptitude of colonial youths for the sea became a
commonplace of the early nineteenth century; 'many of the native
youths', wrote Commissioner Bigge, 'have evinced a strong disposition for a seafaring life, and are excellent sailors'.

There were certain conditions that a staple commodity must
satisfy and which none of those mentioned could satisy. Colonies
founded and maintained with British money must serve the purposes
of the homeland. In its beginnings, at least, the staple must appear
compatible with the penal purposes for which the colonies had been
founded; it must hurt no powerful interest at home unless it served
one still more powerful; and, to attract capital, it must supply some
need in the imperial economy. The best thing would be, as Sir

Joseph Banks put it, 'some native raw material of importance to a manufacturing country such as England is'.

Colonial wool filled all these conditions. Tastes had changed and the demand was now for fine long-stapled wools in place of the traditional short wools that had been grown in England. Unable to sell its products at a profit, English wool-growing declined, and manufacturers were forced into increasing dependence on the fine wools of Spain and Saxony and Silesia. If the colonies could supply such wool, cheaply and in adequate quantities, they would find an avid market in England.

In the demonstration of the promise of colonial fine wools, John Macarthur stands pre-eminent. He was not the only person to interest himself in sheep; but he had the strength of will to resist the temptation of the local commissariat market to breed for mutton, and the intelligence to see that the advantages of the climate must be supported by careful breeding. As early as 1801, the specimens of fine wool which he took to England aroused the interest of English manufacturers; and he returned from England in 1805 with an instruction from the Colonial Secretary, Lord Camden, that he was to be given an unconditional grant of 5,000 acres and the labour of thirty convicts in order to carry on his experiments.

This was a foretaste of a new interest in the Australian colonies. It is true, however, that the change in attitude was slow, just as the demonstration of the promise of Australian merinos was slow.

As late as 1819, when Lord Bathurst sent Commissioner J. T. Bigge to New South Wales, Macarthur was still almost the only pastoralist with pure merino flocks, most of the other breeders having tried to combine mutton and wool. There were still only 100,000 sheep in New South Wales, and they were mostly of poor type. Only 11,000 of them were in the good pastoral land beyond the Blue Mountains, despite the fact that this range had been crossed six years earlier when Blaxland, Lawson and Wentworth kept to the ridges instead of attempting to penetrate the steep-walled imprisoning valleys.

Indeed, at this time the penal usefulness and commercial promise of the colonies stood in balance. The service of the colonies as receptacles for convicts had not waned with the increase of their free people and their free enterprises. Rather, it had grown, for the peace had brought an increase in civilian crime and an increase in the rate at which convicts were transported to the colonies. Almost twice as many prisoners arrived during Macquarie's twelve years as governor (1809–21) as had arrived during the preceding twenty-one years.

On the other hand, there were increasing signs of impatience in the colonies with those irksome restrictions on movement and enterprise that were native to a gaol. For example, in 1819 some 1,250 merchants and settlers, including the leading emancipists of the colony, petitioned the Crown for trial by jury and the lifting of restrictions on colonial trade. They set out the special disabilities affecting the whole range of colonial economic life from agriculture to shipping and the South Seas fishery, and, in the year when Macarthur was complaining that his experiments were little noticed, spoke of the time 'when fine Merino wool will become our principal export to our Mother Country'.

So they drew attention to 'the disabilities, restraints and inconveniences under which the inhabitants of this His Majesty's peculiarly British rising colony labours with regard to the insufficiency of its jurisprudence, the obstructions to its agriculture, the impediments to its navigation with our Mother Country, the operation of the duties applying to its productions imported to England, as well as of those colonial duties imposed on its exports here'. In all these matters, they asked to be put on the same footing as His Majesty's other colonies. That petition did not go unheard, and the next few years saw a partial lifting of the restrictions on trade and a partial concession of civil rights.

For this period of Lachlan Macquarie's governorship (1809–21) was one of rapid growth. Though absolute numbers might still seem small, the increase was marked in the number of people and of their flocks and herds, their acres of cultivated and pasture land, their roads and buildings, their wharves and ships. The stepping-up of transportation played its part in this expansion by increasing the supply both of labour and of capital in the form of government expenditure on the convict establishment. Macquarie, a great builder, used his opportunity to provide the colony with roads and wharves and buildings of a dignity and solidity worthy of something better than a gaol. Sydney and Hobart were beginning to take on an air of settled permanence.

It was in keeping with the state of progresss in the colonies that official policy in England was also hesitating between penal and commercial aims. In 1819, Lord Bathurst sent J. T. Bigge to inquire into the state of New South Wales and Van Diemen's Land, and gave him two sets of instructions which made this hesitation evident. The first reminded him that the settlements had been founded for penal ends; 'they must chiefly be considered as receptacles for offenders' and it was necessary to maintain in New South Wales 'such a system of just discipline as may render transportation an object of serious apprehension'. But the second informed him that the day might come when transportation would cease, and required him to report, though separately, on the development of those settlements as colonies.

On the former subject, Bigge was bound by his instructions and by his somewhat limited imagination to be out of sympathy with Macquarie's attempts to reform by clemency and to break down the rule of caste which the 'exclusive' free settlers would have imposed. But his report 'On the State of Agriculture and Trade in New South Wales', which answered his second instruction, gave an impressive picture of the varied commercial possibilities of the colonies.

It is true that he reported, as he was required to report, on the danger to convict discipline of removing those restrictions on the movements of vessels which were designed to prevent convicts from escaping. It is true, also, that he saw the economic prospects of the colonies through the eyes of men like Macarthur, and that his reports favoured the big man rather than the small. But in this he was true to the facts. Colonial circumstances as well as colonial history were adverse to the small man, and the hope of a growing free economy was then with the capitalist. What he saw as he moved about the country was the almost universal dilapidation and improvidence of small holdings, and the fact that improvement and experiment were of necessity the work of substantial landowners.

He saw the promise of the pastoral industry clearly. 'Upon the expediency', he wrote, 'of promoting in the colony of New South Wales the growth of fine wool, and creating a valuable export from thence to Great Britain, no doubt can be entertained.' Seeing wool as the colony's coming staple, he was bound to look at the colony's future through the eyes of the wool growers. It is true that in doing so he went further than facts required, and saw Macquarie's humane administration with the bias of large settlers whose social prejudice and whose excessive demands for more than their share of the limited number of skilled convicts Macquarie had been obliged to resist.

Bigge saw a way to combine both penal and commercial purposes. It was, in fact, a way proposed to him by Macarthur. Let men of capital be encouraged by grants of land in proportion to capital and by the reduction of imperial duties on colonial wool, and let the convicts be taken away from the temptations of seaports and towns and dispersed as servants to these men of capital in the interior. Such in rough outline was his recommendation, as to these subjects of report, and such in general was the official policy adopted in the 'twenties.

So the rapid development of the pastoral economy of New South

Wales was aided by an extension of the assignment system, while
duties on colonial wool were suspended in 1825 and those on other
colonial goods reduced. The old policy of making small grants of
land to emancipists and poor immigrants was finally abandoned,
and was replaced piecemeal by new land policies which were designed
to attract men of capital to the colony. The stage was set for the
pastoral expansion of the 'twenties.

From this time the commercial importance of the colonies steadily
outstripped their service as places of punishment. In 1821, the year
of the first commerical export of Australian wool, only 175,400
pounds had been sent to England. In 1830, 2,000,000 pounds were
exported, a figure which rose to 10,000,000 in 1839 and to 24,000,000
in 1845. By 1850 the Australian colonies were supplying more fine
wool to English manufacturers than Germany and Spain together.
The Australian proportion of British imports fell during the next
decade when woollen manufacturers grew more rapidly than the
Australian clip; but by 1865, Australian sheep were once again
supplying more than half England's imported wool and were moving
strongly into the position of unchallenged supremacy which they
have retained to this day.

Those thirty years after 1820 saw a rising tide of British investment
in the colonies. It was no doubt a trickle compared with the flow
of British capital to North America; but it was sufficient to transform
the colonial economy.

The general character of this investment is clear in the foundation
in 1824–5 of two chartered land companies each with a capital of
£1,000,000, the Australian Agricultural Company and the Van
Diemen's Land Company; in the many banks and insurance companies of the 'twenties and 'thirties concerned mainly with the
colonial woollen trade; in the new schemes of speculative colonization which founded new colonies in Western and South Australia
and spread the bounds of pastoral settlement in the old; and in the
immigration of people of large or small means in numbers far
greater than in earlier years.

The colonies had come to have a new importance in the eyes of
both governments and subjects. No longer mere receptacles for the
outcasts of society, they were attractive both to capital and to capitalists.

It was inevitable that this change in their character should be
accompanied by a change in their form of government.

Until 1823 New South Wales was ruled by a governor unchecked
by any council. Van Diemen's Land, technically part of New South
Wales, was separately administered by a lieutenant-governor who

was in a general way responsible to the governor of the older colony. The governor's powers were extremely vague and their legality open to question. From the beginning he was simply obliged to assume wide discretion in issuing regulations with the force of law and in imposing duties and taxes.

In a penal colony, a large proportion of the governor's regulations were bound to be of a restrictive type, intended to preserve convict discipline. As the number of free people and the scale of their business grew, such regulations were found increasingly irksome. So Lord Bathurst wrote in 1817 when he was proposing the commission of inquiry into the state of the penal colonies:

The settlers feel a repugnance to submit to the enforcement of regulations which, necessarily partaking much of the nature of the rules applicable to a penitentiary, interfere materially with the exercise of those rights which they enjoyed in this country, and to which as British subjects they conceive themselves entitled in every part of His Majesty's dominions.

The hostility of free settlers to the autocratic rule of the governor was no new thing when Bathurst took this note of it. Hunter, King and Bligh had ruled in stormy conflict with the members of the rum ring. Macquarie's governorship continued the tradition of conflict in his quarrels with the 'exclusives', the wealthy free settlers who included former members of that monopoly. The early opposition to the governors contained no constructive quality, no germ of constitutional government, but remained particular and personal, relying on the influence of powerful friends at home with the British Government to defeat those actions of the colonial governors which were disliked.

Indeed, the only general division of the community in which some conflict of principle might be discerned was that between the exclusives and the emancipists. It was inevitable in a penal colony that the always free should be acutely conscious of their moral superiority. The social exclusiveness of the age was exaggerated by this fact and threatened colonial society with a repressive rule of caste. Macquarie incurred the wrath of the exclusives by his attempts to restore to the dignity of free men in all walks of colonial life those emancipists whom he thought, not always wisely, to be worthy of his help. 'The circumstance', complained Macarthur, 'of having come free to the colony, conferred no claim to favour; and that of having been convicted became proverbially the best security for preferment.'

The emancipists on their side had no reason to form a party of political oppostition, for the governors had consistently been their protectors against the corps and against the exclusives. Their needs

were not political but legal. They regarded the existing courts as
biased against them and wanted trial by jury so that they might be
tried by people free from exclusive prejudice. And, after a legal
decision of 1820 which had thrown their status, and particularly
their right to hold and convey property, into doubt, they wanted
their restoration to the full civil rights of free persons to be confirmed.

One of Bathurst's objects in sending Commissioner Bigge to the
colonies had been to gain information on which to base a reconstruction of their government. This was carried out by an Act of Parliament of 1823 which established a nominated council of from five to
seven members to advise the governor. It confirmed his power, with
that advice, to make laws; but it contained an important provision
that he must first gain from the chief justice of the colony a certificate
that a proposed law was not repugnant to the laws of England so far
as the circumstances of the colony would admit. It further removed
the legal disabilities of which the emancipists had complained, though
trial by jury was not fully gained until 1839. A further step was taken
in 1828 when the nominated council was slightly enlarged, and given
rather more power to check the governor's powers of legislation.

The councils established by these Acts were not concessions to
colonial agitation, but means of giving validity to the governor's
legislation. Colonial agitation for self-government through elected
assemblies does not become at all general until the 1830s, when their
opposition to the land policies of the British Government gave the
colonists for the first time a general ground of political action.

Meanwhile, the governor remained in the unhappy position of an
autocrat who lacked the autocrat's personal freedom of decision. He
was responsible to more than one department of state at home, to
the Colonial Office for general administration, to the Home Secretary
for the convict establishment, and to the Secretary for War for the
military establishment. He might at times influence general policy
but he was often forced to carry out unpopular policies to which he
was personally opposed. Since he could not be controlled by those he
ruled, he was inevitably, even in such cases, the object of attack on
colonial platforms and in the violent colonial press. His officials
were rarely of his own choosing, and many a governor ruled less by
the help of his officials than in spite of their obstruction.

These various disadvantages reached their height in the 'thirties
and 'forties. For by this time, the Colonial Office had evolved a
colonial policy, while the colonies had grown to the point of having
powerful and organized local interests which found themselves in
conflict with that policy. It was a position which could be resolved
only by the granting of responsible government.

5

EXPERIMENTAL COLONIZATION

Meanwhile, the penal character of Australian colonization was being diluted by the foundation of experimental free colonies in Western and South Australia, by the increase of free immigration, and by the pastoral occupation of those outlying parts of New South Wales which were to become the colonies of Victoria and Queensland.

The foundation of experimental colonies and the expansion of the old drew in common on the mother country both for people and for capital. While much of this capital was absentee investment, much of it came as the savings, small or large, of people who saw fit to come out in person to the colonies. How much was brought in in this way cannot be more than guessed. Certainly it played a proportionately greater role at that time than in the latter half of the century when loans floated in London by colonial governments provided the greater part of imported colonial capital.

The coming to Australia of people having enough money to set themselves up in independent livelihoods has a social significance beyond the swelling of the colonial supply of capital. There has been no complete study of Australia's middle-class immigrants and of the causes of their emigration. It is clear they left home because of actual or foreseen difficulties as much as because of colonial prospects. National income was growing, but it was doing so by a process of economic change which hit not only the labouring classes but many people above them in the economic and social scale.

Some of our moneyed immigrants were small gentry who suffered from the decline of wool growing at home, while the post-war vicissitudes of British agriculture uprooted many farmers and small landowners, as well as townspeople dealing in agricultural produce. Clapham writes of 'the savage fluctuations of the grain trade' in this period. Beyond all these, in a time of declining infant and maternal mortality, were the more numerously surviving children of large Victorian families whose parents hoped that the small capital they could provide their growing sons would give them a better start in the colonies than at home. Many a vicar's son was to be found among these middle-class immigrants. Another fairly numerous group consisted of army officers, particularly from India, when military establishments were being cut down by both the British Government and the East India Company.

For one reason and another, many people of more or less comfortable station were faced with a decline in both comfort and status which they might hope to avoid by emigration. It is this situation which probably contributed most to that amazingly simple optimism with which so many left home. Once the momentous decision had been taken to tear up one's roots from the familiar soil, it was human nature to magnify the hopes which supported that decision and to still the doubts which seemed to question its wisdom. They might watch with heavy hearts as the chalk cliffs faded; but, the parting over, their thoughts turned to the colonies as to the promised land.

Though in time success came to many, and a sense of release and freedom to more, the colonies were inevitably unlike their vague if picturesque imaginings, and the first experience was often one of frustration. The irritability, so often remarked, of colonial society and especially of colonial politics no doubt owed something to this. Frustration, however, came later; the initial mood of emigration was one of facile optimism, with whatever personal regrets it might be intermingled.

That same optimism was shared by the larger people, the commercial speculators, the philanthropists and the colonial theorists, who sponsored the new colonies of Swan River and South Australia. In 1827 Captain James Stirling examined the Swan River on the west coast of New Holland; his glowing account was sufficient, without other confirmation, to inspire a syndicate of Thomas Peel and three other capitalists to plan a speculative colony at that place. So, again, the news in 1830 of Captain Sturt's discovery of good land in South Australia was quite sufficient to decide the Wakefieldian theorists that this should be the site of their experimental colony.

Governments needed more persuading. Officials of the Colonial Office knew from sad experience that colonies were in the habit of proving costly to the Treasury. Nevertheless, it was official policy to hold the entire continent against possible foreign intruders and to reserve its future benefits for the British nation. Suspicions of French designs had inspired the precautionary settlement of Van

Diemen's Land in 1803–4. So, twenty years later, renewed fears of
French activity in Australian waters and of the expansion of the
Dutch towards Australia in their islands to the north of it occasioned
a further bout of precautionary colonization—two short-lived settlements at Melville Island on the north-western coast of the continent
and at Westernport on its south-eastern coast, and an enduring
garrison settlement at Albany on King George's Sound in Western
Australia.

The conflict between the desire to avoid expense and the desire to
hold the continent made for ineffective compromise. The proposals
of speculative and theoretical colonizers were not rejected, but their
terms were whittled down to the point of courting failure.

New settlements require a great deal of preliminary work and
expenditure before profitable production can overtake the initial
outlay. Before their commercial promise had been proved, the penal
settlements at Sydney and in Van Diemen's Land had been saved
from collapse by government expenditure in provisioning, housing
and paying the civil, military and convict establishments. This
expenditure had given the colonists maintenance and a market,
while the convicts provided them with labour, until time allowed
local industry to produce articles for export and to attract private
capital and free labour.

In a manuscript note of 1806 on 'the present state of the Colony
of Sidney', Sir Joseph Banks had recognized this as a natural incident
of new settlements: 'The Colony of Sidney at its first establishment
may not unaptly be compared to a new-born infant hanging at its
Mother's breast, it derived its whole nourishment from the Vitals of
its Parent. . . .'

The experimental settlements of the Swan River and South Australia might seek their nourishment of capital from three sources—
government expenditure, speculative investment and the savings of
the settlers. The grudging agreement of the government to these
ventures made it certain that government expenditure would be small
or absent. A common underestimation of the preliminary costs and
labour of mass settlement had the effect that in both schemes private
capital was also inadequate.

This failure to compute the cost and difficulty of colonization is a
recurrent theme in colonial history. It is in part simply the optimism
of times of commercial expansion. But in the case of these two
settlements, easy confidence owed something to philanthropic and
theoretical idealism; enraptured by the goodness of the ends they
looked to, colonial theorists readily imagined that the means were
not difficult.

In the earlier settlement, that on Swan River, commercial speculation was a stronger ingredient than philanthropy, and the proposals
of Peels' syndicate obviously looked back to the large grants of land
made only a few years earlier to the two chartered companies in the
eastern colonies, the Australian Agricultural Company, and the
Van Diemen's Land Company. But even here philanthropy had its
place; Peel's proposal to ship some 10,000 people in four years to the
Swan appealed to the prevalent fear of over-population. In the year
of that proposal, 1827, the first of a number of select committees on
population had reported on emigration as a means of removing the
surplus poor. In the South Australian settlement, as we shall see,
theory and idealism played a much greater part.

The proposal of Peel's syndicate was that it should receive a grant
in monopoly of 4,000,000 acres in the Swan River area on condition
that it spent £300,000, one shilling and sixpence an acre, in sending
out 10,000 settlers with stock. The government reduced the grant to
1,000,000 acres and refused the monopoly on which the syndicate
depended for financial success. The same right was allowed to any
private settler who cared to go, to take up land at the rate of one
acre for every one and sixpence of his capital. Peel's three companies
withdrew; but Peel let hope outrun discretion and accepted these
terms, ruining himself in the process.

The hope of sufficient endowment from speculative capital
disappeared with the withdrawal of Peel's companions. The government sent out a civil and military establishment under Captain
Stirling as governor. It was well chosen, but small; and the policy
was to incur no avoidable expense. It was clear that the new colony
would receive no sufficient nourishment from government expenditure. The remaining source of capital was that brought out with them
by the settlers, including Peel and the £50,000 which he put into the
venture. Here again the amount was far less than the need, and the
contrast was sharp between easy hopes and difficulties actually
encountered.

This was no developed colony with land already cleared, and
wharves, roads and bridges, timber yards and brick yards, ready for
use. The preliminary survey, it is true, was carried out quickly and
simply. But there was much to do before settlers could get themselves,
their stock and their equipment from ship to holding over trackless
country, and much more to do to turn the wild bush into smiling
farms. A few settlers had accompanied Stirling's official party, and
others arrived in quick succession before the most elementary
preparations could be made for their reception. It was the first shock
to high hopes to be forced to camp primitively while the survey was

pushed ahead and land allotted, and a greater one to be forced to leave treasured goods on the beach through lack of roads and cartage to carry them inland.

That first failure to realize the size of their task in breaking in new country might have caused no more than a temporary depression of hope if the settlers had possessed sufficient capital to employ their labourers and develop their holdings when they received them. But the case of Thomas Peel wrote in large letters a common failure of the settlers to estimate the capital cost of their venture. Peel had used £50,000 to bring out 300 labourers and stock; but he had left himself too little capital to maintain and employ the workmen whose passages he had paid. He was obliged to free from their indentures those who had not already absconded, and to retire to a lonely and primitive existence in a stone hut on his large and undeveloped estate south of Perth.

It was the general story that the moneyed colonists had left themselves too little capital to improve their lands once acquired. Charles Bussell, a member of a sturdy and vigorous family of pioneers who settled south of the Swan, estimated that £800 was too little to establish a settler on the land even in a small way. Many with quite large estates had less.

Unable to feed or pay their labourers, they were forced to a large extent to release them from their indentures. They had been unwisely chosen from the workhouses in any case and proved too often unworthy of their hire. So, having come to the Swan with thoughts of a cultured life as landowners employing labour, the moneyed settlers had themselves to turn, men, women and children, to grubbing out trees, cultivating an ungenerous soil and tending their stock; or, if shaped in tenderer, or perhaps less obstinate moulds, they cut their losses and sought an easier living at home or in the more developed eastern colonies. It is the obverse of this ruin of easy hopes that so many men and women, though unused to manual labour, drew on courage, adaptability and endurance to carry them through hardship to success.

There were other difficulties. Swan River did not confirm the favourable accounts that had been given of it. The limestone and sandy soils of the coastal plain were poor. To the south, the immense hardwood forests of the timber country, a future source of wealth, opposed inconceivable obstacles to first settlers. The Darling Ranges east of Perth held pockets of good soil; but required great labour in clearing dense forest. Beyond the ranges some of Western Australia's small proportion of good land was early discovered in the York district; but here also successful cultivation required the clearing of scrub and the building of roads and bridges which again pointed to the colony's insufficiency of capital for preliminary development.

A direct result of these conditions was a wide dispersion of settlement. This in turn increased the costs and difficulties of marketing produce, and enlarged the need for extensive road and bridge building which the colonists could ill afford. Edward Gibbon Wakefield did not tire of condemning this dispersion and ascribing it to the easy terms on which land was granted. These terms did encourage the acquisition of large estates and a consequent scattering of settlement; but this was, in any case, dictated by the necessity to seek out the widely separated pockets of good land. It is true, however, that the easy acquisition of land checked the sale of crown lands when this system replaced grants in 1834, and thereby destroyed the prospect of a revenue from land sales which might provide public equipment and bring out labourers.

For all these reasons, the colony languished for twenty years until in desperation the colonists asked for and received convicts from Great Britain, with the expenditure of British money on the convict establishments which accompanied that doubtful gift. Convict gangs built the roads and bridges and public buildings which the colony needed. Both the 10,000 convicts sent out between 1850 and 1868, and the free labourers sent with them to dilute the tainted stream, swelled the supply of private labour. The expenditure of £2,000,000 on the convict establishment increased the colony's capital for development.

So it entered into a period of more stable growth. In those same years, exploration and improved land laws encouraged a spread of settlement and a stronger development of primary industries. In the 'sixties, the pastoral occupation of the north-west approached the tropic of Capricorn, and its possibilities, sometimes greatly exaggerated, attracted immigrants and investment from the more fully developed eastern colonies. Some of those immigrants joined in ventures which repeated all the old optimism and all the old mistakes of the original settlement.

In the course of this growth through trials and difficulties, the colonists developed a neighbourliness which the eastern visitor still observes; for only in the 1960s did Western Australian industries reach the scale that counters the colonial tradition with the tensions of industrial society.

The Swan River Colony was founded in the year in which Edward Gibbon Wakefield's *Letter from Sydney* was published. In it he first expounded the theory of systematic colonization which proposed to remedy the chronic labour shortage and the straggling crudity of colonial settlement by means of the mechanism of 'the sufficient price'.

Wakefield wrote his *Letter from Sydney* in the assumed character of an immigrant of fortune who had bought 20,000 acres for no more than two shillings an acre. 'As my estate cost me next to nothing, so it is worth next to nothing. . . . Having fortune enough for all my wants, I proposed to get a large domain, to build a good house, to keep enough land in my own hands for pleasure-grounds, park, and game preserves; and to let the rest, after erecting farm-houses in the most suitable spots. My mansion, park, preserves, and tenants were all a mere dream. I have not one of them.'

For labourers could not be found to build his buildings, nor tenants to occupy his farms. Since land was so easily obtained that labourers soon became landowners, labour was scarce and wages were high. One may comment that land was not then so easily obtained by a labourer as Wakefield thought; but labour was always scarce and expensive in expanding colonies.

Wakefield's remedy was to sell land at a 'sufficient price'. He did not name this price; but it should be fixed and uniform, considerable and determined by experience. It must not be so high as to put a stop to the sale of land; but it should preserve a due proportion between land and the supply of labour by preventing labourers from becoming landowners in less, say, than six years. It would serve its purpose even if the proceeds of land sales were thrown into the sea; but it could be made to swell the labour supply if these proceeds were used to pay the fares of labouring immigrants from the mother country.

The sufficient price would do more. It would transform colonial makeshift into civilization. For plentiful labour would enable the landowner to cultivate not only his land but the arts of leisure. So the colonies would become more attractive to men of means and education. And the high price of land would prevent the scattering of settlement and promote those amenities and pursuits of civilization which could appear only where people were settled close together.

We are in a barbarous condition [he wrote, still in the guise of a settler in New South Wales], like that of every people scattered over a territory immense in proportion to their numbers; every man is obliged to occupy himself with questions of daily bread; there is neither leisure nor reward for the investigation of abstract truth; money-getting is the universal object; taste, science, morals, manners, abstract politics, are subjects of little interest, unless they happen to bear upon the wool question; and, what is more deplorable, we have not any prospect of a change for the better. . . . Here we have nothing but wool, wool, wool.

The colonists with their faith in wool were living in a fool's paradise, he believed; for over-production would glut the market. Wool monopolized the stage only because, in a country of cheap land and dear labour, wool had for the time being the advantage that it required much land and little labour. Once reverse the proportions, so that land became moderately dear and labour moderately cheap, and wool would lose its monopoly, and allow, at least side by side with it, the concentrated settlement that was indispensable to civilization. Then his dream might become reality, and it was to re-create old England, without its paupers, in the sunny if not very green land of New South Wales. 'The colonies . . . would no longer be new societies, strictly speaking. They would be so many extensions of an old society.'

This new England under southern skies was an England seen through the eyes of a liberal colonial reformer, who was to influence the Durham Report. It was, therefore, to be a self-governing society, enjoying the free institutions of English men. But a self-governing society could not also be a penal colony, nor did Wakefield regard convicts as satisfactory labourers. Labour must not only be plentiful; it must also be respectable and self-respecting. Careful selection of labouring immigrants was one of the pillars of his system.

The theory had its share of fallacy. But its influence on colonial policy, if sometimes exaggerated, was important to the colonies of Australia and New Zealand, That influence, in so far as it raised the price of crown land, stirred the colonists to a dislike of Wakefieldians in particular and of colonial theorists in general. But Wakefieldian propaganda at least hastened the ending of transportation and the granting of free institutions. Moreover, South Australia was settled as a demonstration of 'systematic colonization' and the model was improved on in the Wakefieldian settlements of New Zealand. Further, the schemes of assisted immigration financed from land sales were the direct, and, for Australia, the most enduring result of Wakefield's work.

At this time the condition of 'the redundant poor' of the British Isles was the source of great misery to themselves and of growing anxiety to governments and charitable organizations. Irish conditions were particularly distressing. The Irish, declared the Select Committee on Emigration of 1826–7, 'unless some other outlet be opened to them, must shortly fill up every vacuum created in England or in Scotland, and reduce the labouring classes to a uniform state of degradation and misery'.

The colonies on the other hand were crying out for labour.

C

Emigration was the obvious cure for Britain's surplus and the colonies' shortage. And, indeed, though the British Isles were yet to support many more millions than they held in 1826, emigration seemed at that time an inescapable necessity for the happiness and good order of the community and the preservation of its living standards. Close on 3,000,000 people emigrated from Great Britain between 1825 and 1851.

The Australian colonies, however, were at a great disadvantage in the competition for immigrants. The voyage of 12,000 miles or more to the under parts of the earth was both longer and more costly than the crossing of the Atlantic to the North American colonies and the United States. The emigrant to Australia must expect to spend four or five months at sea, as compared with twelve weeks to Canada; and his passage would cost him £20 or £25 instead of £5 to Canada. Nor were the penal taint and strangeness of the antipodean colonies balanced by any promise of greater opportunity for the labourer than he could find, in his own hemisphere, on the other side of the Atlantic.

The contribution of Wakefield is that his proposal to use the land fund to pay the passages of labourers eliminated the one disadvantage of cost. It could not balance the greater appeal of North America in other respects; and in the years 1825–52, over two and a half million people sailed from Great Britain to the United States, while only 223,000 took the longer journey to Australia and New Zealand. But the offer of assistance did net some portion of the shoal of emigration which was removing the redundant population of the British Isles.

If the assisted immigrants brought out under official schemes after 1831 included a large proportion of pauperized and broken people from workhouses and institutions, they were the best that distant Australia could attract; or, at least, they were so after the methods of selection had been improved in the mid-thirties. Colonial criticism of the assisted immigrants was unrestrained, and, in the early years of lax selection, justified. But immigrants coming from conditions of poverty have always been resented, and those same immigrants have often enough resented in their turn the newcomers of a later generation.

Criticism owed something to the colonial tradition of forced labour; for some of the immigrants, coming from English Chartism and Irish unrest, proved less docile than convict servants. Poor as their general quality may have been, many of them were people of character and intelligence, and some, such as Henry Parkes, later Premier of New South Wales, were of outstanding quality.

There were also special schemes of assisted immigration conducted by non-government bodies and by individuals such as Caroline Chisholm and John Dunmore Lang. Caroline Chisholm and Lang were as much concerned with colonial morals as with the colonial labour supply, and tried to bring a leaven of virtue into the vicious society of the penal colonies. Lang's 'decent Scots mechanics' and Caroline Chisholm's scheme of 'family colonization' with its women and children as 'God's police', were means to a moral as much as to an economic end.

Assisted immigration was an aspect of Wakefieldian theory which could be applied to existing colonies; but the theory required an unspoilt field for its demonstration as a whole. News in 1830 of Captain Sturt's discovery of good land in South Australia suggested a site for an experimental colony. In time, public propaganda and private lobbying wore down the government's resistance, and in 1834 a foundation act was passed to establish the British Province of South Australia. The first settlers arrived two years later in 1836.

The projectors of this new colony could not overlook the difficulties then besetting the Swan River Colony. But the trials of the Swan were regarded as evidence of the folly of unsystematic colonization and, in reverse, as evidence for the wisdom of systematic colonization on Wakefield's principles. Yet these two examples of colonization had much in common, despite the contrast made between them at that time and so often since.

In both schemes, commercial speculation was mixed with a public idealism. Into both there entered an optimism too little calculating. In both cases the British Government resisted the first proposals, allowing its resistance to be worn down at length into grudging compromise.

Public idealism was particularly evident in the South Australian venture. Indifferent as the great majority of people might be to Wakefield's theories, there were those in his following who looked upon his ideas as nothing less than the key to a new era of happy and prosperous colonization. Such faith promoted an excess of optimism. The scheme was the more attractive because it was supposed that a colony founded on Wakefield's principles would be less outlandish and more like home than the unfavourably contrasted penal colonies. 'A colony so founded,' Archbishop Whateley declared, 'would fairly represent English society. . . . There would be little more revolting to the feelings of an emigrant than if he had merely shifted his residence from Sussex to Cumberland or Devonshire.'

The troubles of the Swan River colonists did not shake this easy faith; commercial optimism at a time of expansion is scarce so strong as the common readiness to expect much from political devices, and

Wakefield's sufficient price was a device that won the unquestioning support of his adherents.

Government did not share this optimism. The colony was permitted, but only on condition that it should not be a charge on the exchequer. The Government was to be no wet nurse to an infant whose birth it countenanced without favour. The effect of this condition was to deprive the new settlement of the government expenditure which, at least in Australia, mass settlement in virgin country had not yet been able to do without.

The capital costs of establishing the settlement must, therefore, come from private sources; and here also the similarity with the Swan River settlement holds, in that the promoters of the South Australian scheme underestimated the preliminary cost and labour of establishing a new colony, betraying their facile optimism in glib talk of 'self supporting colonization'. This was a mistake which Wakefield did not share.

Yet the South Australian settlement began with certain advantages over the Swan River settlement. Some of these advantages stand to the credit of Wakefieldian theory. In accordance with his principles, labouring immigrants were more carefully selected than they had been for the Swan, and they proved the value of this initial care. And, though Wakefield thought it too low, the comparatively high price of twelve shillings an acre at which land was to be sold in the new settlement kept away would-be settlers with insufficient capital to establish themselves. The South Australian venture like that on the Swan River came near to failure through the insufficiency of its preliminary public expenditure; but that insufficiency did not in general extend to its private settlers.

Moreover, considerable private capital was brought into the colony by the South Australian Company, a speculative venture formed by George Fife Angas and a group of capitalists who invested £320,000 in the scheme. This company successfully played the role in South Australia which Peel had so sadly failed to play in the west, and it did much to save the new settlement in its early struggles.

Greatest of all the advantages which distinguished South Australian settlement was the proximity of good wheat lands close to the sea and close to the centre of settlement. Their profitable use did not have to wait, as did the use of the inland wheat belts of western and eastern Australia, until the building of railways cheapened freights. Moreover, if the soil was not exceptionally fertile, it was both better and more uniform than that of the Swan River district. It could be divided in smaller and more compact holdings which could be worked profitably even at the comparatively high price at which it was sold to the settlers. That price would have imposed an impossible burden in the poorer and streakier lands of Western Australia. In South Australia, at least, nature smiled on systematic colonization and on its principle of concentration.

Despite such advantages, the new foundation came close to disaster. The foundation act divided authority between a governor responsible to the Colonial Office and a resident-commissioner who was responsible to a non-government board of commissioners in London. This board held the power of the purse and therefore the final control of policy. But the friction between the two authorities was an irritant and a hindrance to the solution of the colony's difficulties rather than their cause.

The main cause of those difficulties was the commissioners' failure to understand the preliminary cost and labour of that task of mass settlement which they had undertaken in the optimistic mood of 'self-supporting colonization'. So the main lessons of Swan River were not learnt, and some of its worst errors were repeated. It is true that the commissioners' resources were limited since they could not draw on the treasury and could raise loans only up to a limit of £200,000, while the land fund was earmarked to meet the costs of assisted immigration. But they failed to use those resources which they could use quickly enough to get their settlers on to the land and into production.

They were for the most part inexperienced, and Wakefield, who quarrelled with them, called them 'ignorant and careless amateurs'. Indeed, Wakefield disagreed with them on a number of points and refused to regard South Australia as a test of his theory. Yet it may well be that the commissioners' inexperience was the less redeemed by imagination because their attachment to his theory, if not complete enough to satisfy Wakefield, was enough to check adaptation to unforeseen circumstance.

Their first mistake was to make the task of their surveyor-general, William Light, impossible. He was sent to the projected site of settlement only a few months in advance of the main body of settlers and required to carry out a peculiarly elaborate form of survey with insufficient men and transport. When his requests for additional help were met by carping criticism, he resigned, and the survey, the prerequisite of settlement, came almost to a standstill. When later it was resumed, it cost the sum he had estimated. As in the Swan River settlement, the colonists were kept waiting inactive; and, unable to begin production, they began an orgy of speculation in town and country lots, easily made money obscuring the fact that such speculation must end in disaster unless production could begin.

So the systematic colony languished like its unsystematic fore-runner on the Swan. In 1839, Colonel George Gawler was sent out to combine the offices of governor and resident-commissioner in his own person. He found few settlers on farms, workmen unemployed, and the colony but little supplied with such necessary equipment as funds, roads or wharves. Scarcely had he arrived when the commissioners poured 8,000 new immigrants into the unprepared colony, for insurrection in Canada had for the moment diverted emigration to Australia.

Gawler saved the colony by pushing ahead with those preliminary works the necessity of which the commissioners had failed to understand. He recruited additional surveyors, and was able by the middle of 1841 to survey half a million acres and to place 5,000 people on the land. Meanwhile, he employed the colony's workmen on necessary public works, providing the roads and buildings which pay no other dividend than the public service without which private production must be hampered. As part of this programme, he allowed tolls and land to the South Australian Company in return for the construction of a deep-water harbour at Port Adelaide.

When he left the colony in 1841, speculation was giving way to production; 7,000 acres were in cultivation and the colony had 200,000 sheep and 15,000 cattle, brought to it for the most part by overlanders from the eastern colonies. It is true that some of his expenditure was lavish and that he might have put the colony on its feet at smaller cost; but it is clear that he did put it on its feet, and in the only way that allowed the unbroken progress that followed.

This achievement had cost more than the colonial revenue at this early stage could pay, and Gawler had used his emergency power to draw bills on the commissioners to an amount £270,000 in excess of revenue. The commissioners themselves had accepted his policy, or at least failed to object to it; but they were replaced at the end of 1839 by a new board which a year later turned in panic to the Government when it failed to raise a loan of £120,000, the residue of the total allowed by the foundation act. As far as its public finance went, and only in this respect, the colony was bankrupt, and Gawler's outstanding bills were for a time dishonoured.

After long delays and a public inquiry, the Government came to the rescue and put the province of South Australia on the normal footing of a crown colony. The young, able and energetic Captain Grey replaced Gawler as governor, with the strict instruction to reduce expenditure by every conceivable means. He did so with ruthless energy. His sudden stopping of public works, dismissal of officials, reduction of wages and raising of taxes caused great distress, and he was burnt in effigy in the streets of Adelaide. But he forced more people out of the town into the country and thereby quickened the pace of development in farming and grazing, while succeeding in his special task of reducing expenditure. His success in both tasks had been made possible by Gawler's preparatory work.

Rising prosperity soon enabled revenue to balance expenditure. Despite all its troubles, South Australia had cost the British Government less than a quatrer of a million pounds—a small subsidy to set beside the achievement of a colony which numbered 17,000 people by 1843 and which was then entering a period of buoyant development. The discovery of copper and silver-lead mines between 1841 and 1845 brought increased prosperity and attracted both capital and immigrants.

For a short time the discovery of gold in 1851 in the neighbouring colonies of New South Wales and Victoria seemed to threaten this prosperity by drawing people away to the gold-fields. But the gold rushes provided South Australian farmers with a suddenly swollen market for their produce. Breadstuffs soon overhauled minerals as the chief South Australian export, and in six years the area under cultivation was more than trebled. South Australian wheat farmers could respond to their opportunity the more readily because a mechanical harvester, Ridley's stripper, invented in South Australia in 1843, had cut the cost of labour in harvesting to one-tenth.

Moreover, much of the direct benefit of Victorian goldmining was drawn to South Australia by a local bullion act which set up a government assay office and fixed the price of gold above the current rate in Melbourne. Much Victorian gold moved overland under escort to South Australia and stimulated investment and development there. The population which had risen to 63,000 in 1850, rose still further to 104,000 in 1856, despite the magnet of the gold-fields.

It was a population more evenly balanced in occupations and wealth than that of any other Australian colony before the gold discoveries. Natural advantages had allowed a rapid development of farming and mining, and pastoralists never gained the isolated predominance in wealth and power which they enjoyed in the eastern colonies.

Its variety attracted immigrants of many types and crafts. Many of them were German Lutherans, assisted by George Fife Angas and other philanthropists to find in South Australia a refuge from persecution. Planting German villages in Australian valleys, they diversified the colony's economy and society with market gardening for the growing population and with small-scale grape growing for a wine industry which was being established in the main by English-men. Other immigrants were brought out by the mining companies, or assisted by the Government from the land fund.

Even before the gold rushes had similar effects in the eastern colonies, South Australian society grew more diverse in status and trade from this immigration, and quite early displayed a varied middle class, the lack of which had made social divisions more strident and more evident in the east. To this degree, Wakefield's ideas were fulfilled; but that fulfilment, if it owed a good deal to his theory, owed still more to the good wheat lands near the sea and to the colony's unpredictable wealth in minerals. Perhaps, too, these facts contributed as much as the early selection of respectable types of immigrants to that sober sense of solid worth that has not ceased to mark South Australian society.

6

PASTORAL SOCIETY

While speculation and theory joined in the foundation of new colonies in Western and South Australia, speculation without theory was planting new settlements within the territory of New South Wales. These were the settlements that were to grow into the colonies of Victoria and Queensland. Their occupation was simply part of the pastoral expansion of the squatting age.

This expansion was spontaneous and against official policy. Even before Wakefield's influence could be felt, the difficulty of policing scattered settlements and a desire to reserve the waste lands of the empire for future generations had given rise to an official policy of concentrated settlement. By 1829 the nineteen counties, from the Manning River south to the Goulburn Plains, and from the coast to the Wellington Valley, had been proclaimed as the limits beyond which settlement must not go in New South Wales. Those who went beyond were, in official eyes, trespassers and outlaws.

It was too late. The promise of the pastoral industry had already been demonstrated, and even as those boundaries were being fixed, squatters were passing beyond them in a search that would continue into the 1880s for 'the good land farther out'. And these 'squatters' on crown land were not the disreputable sheep-stealers and grog-traders to whom that term had earlier been applied, but men of standing and substance. They were trespassers, but their trespass simply had to be allowed. 'As well attempt to confine an Arab within a circle traced on sand,' wrote Governor Gipps in a dispatch of 1840, 'as to confine the graziers or wool growers of New South Wales within bounds that can possibly be assigned to them.'

His predecessor, Governor Bourke, faced with the squatting rush across the boundaries, had come to the same conclusion, and had tried to replace futile prohibition by regulation. Settlement beyond

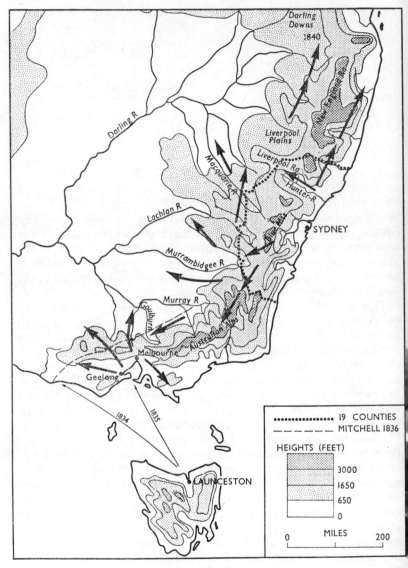

Fig. 2

Fig. 2. The Pastoral Occupation of South Eastern Australia. The Nineteen Counties marked the official limits of settlement in 1829. Arrows show the main directions of pastoral occupation to 1840. The line marked 'Mitchell 1836' ('the Major's Line') was Mitchell's return track. This was a main line of movement to the south. After S. H. Roberts, *The Squatting Age*.

the limits was allowed in 1836 on payment of an annual licence fee of £10. This conferred no right of property, but only a right to graze stock on crown land for the period of the licence. Commissioners of crown lands were appointed who issued the licence, determined by rough and ready means the area to which it applied, and decided disputes as to prior occupancy. In 1839 a variable tax on stock was added to the licence fee.

Meanwhile, pastoral settlement had been stretching far to the north and south of the old nineteen counties.

In 1836 Major Thomas Mitchell explored the rich western district of Victoria. 'Of this Eden', he declared, neglecting both the aborigines and his companions, 'I was the only Adam'. His enthusiastic reports of what he called 'Australian Felix' set in motion a new squatting rush to the south of the Murray River, though even before his journey, some squatters had moved down to the southern side of the Murray. Meanwhile occupation had already begun from Van Diemen's Land, and the Henty brothers from that island had been grazing sheep and whaling for two years at Portland Bay when Mitchell found them there. And, as the explorer looked over the basalt plain from Mt Macedon towards the waters of Port Phillip, other squatters from Van Diemen's Land were already camped on its shores, and their vessels were plying back and forth between Launceston and Port Phillip, bringing over stock, labourers, equipment and provisions.

For the pastoral lands of Van Diemen's Land were fully occupied, and the idea of extending settlement to the north of the straits had been in the air for close on a decade. Their dependence on sea communications and their sealing ventures in Bass Strait had made the Victorian coasts familiar territory to the islanders. The Port Phillip Association, which was the prime mover in the settlement of the area north and west of Port Phillip in 1836, found itself from the outset in competition with other groups and with individual venturers seeking similar opportunity across the straits. In short, the settlement of Victoria was an instance of spontaneous settlement, overland from New South Wales and across the straits from Van Diemen's Land.

If it lacked the admixture of theory and philanthropy which had marked the settlement of Western and South Australia, it shared to the full their character of commercial speculation. The Port Phillip Association included in its fifteen members both pastoralists like John Batman borrowing capital, and financial speculators lending it. Charles Swanston, managing director of the Derwent Bank, may be taken as the type of the latter; for if Batman proposed the idea, Swanston was its architect. He has been described as 'one of a score or so of commercial adventurers who had had at least the illusion of controlling and directing Australian economic expansion in the period during which the emergence of a capitalist economy was completed'.

A captain in the East India Company's forces, he arrived in Hobart in 1831 and set himself up in a great variety of trading and financial business. As an importing agent for firms ranging from Calcutta and Madras to Canton and Manila, he was able to build up a supplementary business as an agent for officers, officials and traders in those parts who wished to invest in colonial enterprises. Through such connections, he attracted investment business on a still larger scale from Great Britain. Both in his private capacity, and as managing director and chief shareholder of the Derwent Bank, he placed the greater part of such investment in pastoral enterprises and in banking ventures which staked their success in the main on pastoral undertakings.

The largest enterprise in which Swanston ventured his own and his clients' savings was the Port Phillip Association. In this case he burnt his own and his clients' fingers. The British Government did not allow the association's claim to some 600,000 acres on the ground of a so-called treaty with the aborigines; and the venture had not overtaken its outlay when the depression years, 1842–6, fell on it. The Port Phillip Bank, a subsidiary of the association, failed and the Derwent Bank was in reality pulled down with it, though it was not wound up until 1854. It was no longer possible to find borrowers at 15 per cent interest, and overseas investors grew more cautious.

Such troubles did not check the rapidity with which Victoria was occupied both by overlanders coming down from the north and by squatters fanning out from Port Phillip. Squatters in difficulties were able to sell their stock and their rights of occupancy to settlers coming direct from Great Britain to the new town of Melbourne. In 1840, after a mere four years of settlement, population exceeded 10,000 and there were 800,000 sheep. By 1847, with the depression between, there were close on 43,000 people and over 4,000,000 sheep while pastoral occupation was spreading into less readily inviting areas. Four years later, on the eve of the gold rushes, there were 77,000 people in the colony of Victoria, with 6,000,000 sheep and close on 400,000 head of cattle on its pastures.

The 'forties saw a similar spread of pastoralists into the southern parts of what was to become in 1859 the colony of Queensland. In this decade, the rich Darling Downs, inland from the penal station established on Moreton Bay in 1824, were occupied by squatters moving north from the New England district of New South Wales.

The steady expansion of the 'fifties accelerated into a great pastoral boom in the 'sixties when sheep and cattle were carried over the inland of Queensland from the border of New South Wales to the Gulf of Carpentaria. For, by this time, attempts in the southern colonies to resume land from the squatters for closer agricultural settlement turned the eyes of pastoralists in those colonies to parts of the continent where unoccupied land might still be found.

The pastoral settlement of Victoria and Queensland differed from the experimental colonization of Western and Southern Australia in yet another respect. Those colonies had been ventures in mass settlement, attempting to create almost at a stroke fairly varied communities dependent in the main on agriculture. The occupation of Port Phillip and Queensland was simply a continuation of the pastoral settlement which had been spreading out from the developed areas of the older colonies. It was the form of colonization which required the least public expenditure on services and equipment.

In the civilian army which occupied Australia the squatters were the advance patrols travelling light. They waited on no survey. Indeed, they sometimes moved in advance of the explorers. Their impedimenta were reduced to bare necessities. Their roads were marked out by the wheels of their bullock-drays, and the bush provided the materials for their sheep-folds and their huts. The port services for handling and shipping and dealing in their wool could be built up piecemeal, as they were needed, by private persons out of the profits to be made from such services. The private cost of establishing a sheep-run was considerable; but the public cost of providing a pastoral community with those services which it could not do without was both smaller and less urgent than in the mass settlements of Swan River and South Australia.

Even before the gold rushes, Victoria had outstripped each of those colonies in population; but population had been attracted—rapidly since Victorian pastures were rich—by the opportunities first created by a thin-spread pastoral occupation. That was the order of settlement which suited the physical environment of a large and dry country, and Port Phillip did not have to appeal to the British Treasury for rescue.

In the course of the pastoral expansion of the squatting age, the first distinctive Australian culture was born. The statement may seem a paradox. For the majority of squatters, being men of small or large capital, but lately come from the middle and upper classes of Great Britain, brought with them the assumptions of leadership, the self-picture of an established rural gentry, and the intellectual tastes and ideas of an older society. In this, they were not marked apart from those squatters who were drawn from the ranks of the wealthier colonial families. Indeed, the idea of a colonial gentry found its best expression in the Camden estate of the Macarthurs and in the native-born William Charles Wentworth's much ridiculed proposal for a colonial house of lords.

A Scottish traveller, John Hood, who visited Australia in 1841 to see his squatter son, has left this description of Camden:

I have passed a most delightful day at C——; a more agreeable English-looking place I have not seen. The house, the park, the water, the gardens, the style of everything and of every person, master and servants, resembled so much what one meets with in the old country, that I could scarcely believe myself sixteen thousand miles from it.

This little island of Europe set in an antipodean wilderness impressed Hood the more vividly as he saw it immediately on returning from the bush where he had found that 'a house seems the last consideration with the bushmen'. Indeed, as he had travelled, the novelty of a new country had worn off; 'there are no links with the past', he wrote, 'no ruins, no reminiscences, no grey hallowed cathedral, no Saxon, no Gothic remnant; when once you have passed the boundaries, there is no temple even of modern erection, whither the people congregate to worship; no green blooming hedges, no green lanes, the beauty and the boast of Britain; no tottering watch-tower to recall the deeds of other days'.

For life in the bush had little in common with the picture of cultured leisure which Hood saw in Camden and which was also Edward Gibbon Wakefield's ideal in the *Letter from Sydney*. Camden Park, when Hood saw it, was the product of half a century's endeavour, and the harshness of acquisition had by that time ripened into the mellowness of inherited wealth.

It is true that it had many companions in the older settled districts of New South Wales and Van Diemen's Land, estates with all the bloom of a cultivated gentry—park-like grounds surrounding homes that had caught something of the dignity and sureness of the regency building to which they owed much. Their quality has been captured by Mr. Hardy Wilson in his *Old Colonial Architecture*. It is also true that in time the rough wooden primitiveness of the first squatting days was to give way to a similar solidity and spaciousness of building and living.

In 1873, Trollope was to write of the larger sheep stations of New South Wales:

The number of sheep at these stations will generally indicate with fair accuracy the mode of life at the head station: 100,000 sheep and upwards require a professed man-cook and a butler to look after them; 40,000 sheep cannot be shorn without a piano; 20,000 is the lowest number that renders napkins at dinner imperative; 10,000 require absolute plenty, meat in plenty, tea in plenty, brandy and water and colonial wine in plenty, but do not expect champagne, sherry, or made dishes, and you are supposed to be content with continued mutton or continued beef—as the squatter may at the time be in the way of killing sheep or oxen.

But how striking at first was the contrast between the dream of solid comfort and the reality! For the main quality of the Squatting Age was the postponement of enjoyment to the present task of acquisition, and its creed was not the civilized amenities of Wakefield's concentrated settlement, but the search for good land farther out. Even when Trollope was writing, that contrast still survived; for at that very time in the north-western district of Western Australia the earlier and more primitive history of squatting was being re-enacted, and you would find no butlers there.

The squatters of eastern Australia in the Squatting Age were drawn from various sources. Some were the sons of established colonists or managers employed by them. Some were colonials of lesser standing—publicans who had grown rich on the colony's endless thirst, or overseers and managers who were able to borrow on the strength of their experience. But a very large proportion of them came to the colonies from overseas with the express purpose of setting up in sheep or cattle. These included a number of army officers when military establishments were being cut down in Great Britain and in India. They were very largely drawn from the professional, business and rural middle-classes of Great Britain, with Scots particularly numerous.

Whatever they were and wherever they came from, they had to own or be able to borrow considerable capital. Gideon Scott Lang in his *Land and Labour in Australia* wrote of them in 1845:

There are two classes into which the capitalists may be divided, first those with a small capital, say £1,500 or £2,000, or more commonly two in company each with half that amount; and second, those with large sums, from £5,000 upwards.

The first are by far the most numerous and form the class by whose exertions the Colony has made such rapid progress. They purchase the largest number of sheep which they can possibly compass and at the same time leave sufficient to provide drays, provisions, etc.; they incur no expense which can by any possibility be avoided, contenting themselves with clothes, provisions, tobacco, etc., the same as their servants, so that they may avoid selling fat sheep or cattle, and be enabled to extend their stock as much as possible before coming in contact with neighbours when they are compelled to make boundaries and limit themselves to these.

They lived 'the same as their servants' because, for most of them, there was no margin left between their capital and the heavy cost of establishing a sheep run. The same writer continued:

To become a perfect specimen of the Australian squatter an emigrant must be a pushing determined fellow, who can dispense with all the comforts of civilized life, from wine and windows to carpets and crockery, and will look to nothing but making the most of his Capital regardless of risk and hardship, so long as they lead to increased profit.

For setting up as a squatter was an expensive business. It cost Edmund Curr £1,500 for the right of occupancy of a wretched run with 2,100 sheep of comparable quality, and over £1,000 for his first year's expenses. At times of inflated costs, as in 1839–40 when sheep fetched as high a price as sixty shillings a head, it might take £5,000 in the first year to establish a run of 1,000 sheep. At any time, the squatter had to be able to lay his hands on a few thousand pounds to begin even in a small way. In general, the wool clip did no more than meet running expenses, and the sale of the increase had to meet payments on borrowed capital and provide any profit. In short, the initial costs were such that the average squatter could not afford permanent building and the comforts of civilized life; and it was not only the insecurity of his tenure which postponed such improvements.

Unless he had large backing, he might lose his capital at the first throw. Unsuccessful squatters left few records; and the tale of failure through the swindling of newcomers by old hands, failure through scab and catarrh in flocks, through drought and flood and fire, through the collapse of prices, all this has to be pieced together from inadequate hints.

F. J. Meyrick's *Life in the Bush, 1840–7*, may balance the more numerous accounts of success. This is the tale of Henry Meyrick, the son of an English vicar. At the age of seventeen years, he came to Port Phillip with a cousin in 1840. Each had £1,000 capital. Staying at the Lamb Inn, they were put wise to things by an old colonial hand. He warned them off sheep; they were too subject to catarrh. He sold them a horse for sixty guineas and poor cattle at similar high prices; and he sent them off to what he described as an ideal place for cattle near Westernport. Six years later, Henry wrote home, 'Had we been in any other part of the country we should now have been independent, but no man can thrive in this accursed

western port. We have worked hard and lived on salt beef and damper for nearly six years to no purpose'.

They moved from bad to worse, from cattle at Westernport to
sheep at Glenmaggie in Gippsland. Crippled with rheumatism, the
lad of twenty-three wrote home: 'It is very much like a large gaol—
twenty-five miles from the nearest squatter, and surrounded for
eight months in the year with snow.' His last letter shows him leaving
Glenmaggie: 'I have no home, no huts, no sheep.' Staying with
friends, he had to cross a flooded river. He came off his horse but
managed to swim to the bank, or almost to it, when he was seen to
turn round and swim out into the middle of the river and sink.

Success required more than hard work. Luck played its part, as
when Edmund Curr, struggling with his wretched holding at Wolfs-
crag, found good land by accident near the Goulburn while he was
searching for lost bullocks. Success could come without previous
knowledge of sheep. Alfred Joyce, whose story is told in *A Homestead
History* edited by G. F. James, arrived in Port Phillip in 1843 and
calculated in 1857 that he had doubled his capital every two and a
half years. When he first set up as a squatter, his 'knowledge of sheep
hitherto had been limited to the butchers' shops or the Smithfield
Market'. But he had a shrewd head for business and his apprentice-
ship in London as a mechanical engineer and millwright had given
him an aptitude in improvised construction which he turned to good
account on his station.

Let us follow the fairly typical progress of a squatter in the early
days. His way might be smoothed with letters of introduction. In
any case, his first need was to buy a horse and ride up country in
search of a run. In the earliest years, he might find unoccupied land
between existing stations, and gain the advantage of known tracks
and neighbours. But he might have to go beyond the farthest limits
of settlement, following the hint of an explorer's journal or exploring
for himself, guided by the gossip of squatters or the report of a
bribed shepherd. In the 'forties, it was becoming usual to purchase
from an earlier squatter the right of occupancy of an existing run
together with its stock and improvements.

Once he had determined on his station, he must return, take out
his licence, hire labour, buy equipment and provisions for a year,
and set out, acquiring sheep or cattle at some convenient point.
These were the days before fencing, and he would need a shepherd for
every 600 or 700 sheep and a hut-keeper for every two or three
shepherds. He would need bullocks and a dray—more than one
dray if his flocks were large—and a bullock-driver to take charge of
it. If he were in a large way he would also require an overseer. He

would have to load the dray with rations for all his party for a year, with wool-packs, shears, tools and other such accessories.

His party might be still larger if he were breaking into new country which might require hard labour in cutting tracks and clearing land. The Leslies, first-comers to the Darling Downs in Queensland, took with them twenty-two ticket-of-leave men and convicts, three drays, two bullock teams, a team of horses and ten saddle horses for their flocks of little over 2,000 sheep.

Once on his run the shepherd king and his men built in a few days the homes that would last them for some years. These were of the flimsiest. Unless his wealth were considerable, the squatter had no margin left for comfort after the purchase of flocks and stores and equipment, and with the wages of his men yet to meet. A sod hut it might be for the squatter, or even the glory of a hut of split slabs with a stone or mud chimney, and a roof of grass thatch or bark. The men's huts were of similar if less substantial type, or, on out-stations, merely a lean-to of boughs or a tarpaulin stretched between the trees.

Rolf Boldrewood in his *Old Melbourne Memories* writes of the western district in the 'forties, 'Then some of the shepherd kings thought it no dishonour to sleep in a watch-box for a month at a time, and a slab gunyah with a fold of hurdles was held to be sufficient improvement for a medium sheep station'.

The watch-box was a roughly made portable box long enough for a man to lie down in. It was placed between the sheep folds and by a large fire at night to accommodate the man who kept watch for the silent ravaging of the dingo, the native dog of Australia, which, if it once penetrated the fold, might destroy twenty or thirty sheep before it was discovered.

Furniture was in keeping with the huts, the product of rough bush carpentry—sapling frames covered with bark or bagging for beds, boxes for table and chairs, some rough shelves for books—for that amenity at least was not discarded—wool-packs suspended for doors inside the hut, sheets of bark for the outside door. Hood describes the 'bark slab door, that turns on the broken end of a black bottle for the lower hinge and is tied with a stirrup-leather for the upper one'. Shutters replaced windows, and in unsettled districts loopholes on either side of the chimney-place served for defence against the attacks of aborigines or bush-rangers.

The pattern was not universal and one might find the cedar furniture of a town house moved to the insecure protection of a slab hut. But in general there was the rough temporariness of bark and slab, a cutting down of all amenities to those which could be gained without further expense by means of the labour and materials available on the spot.

The squatter who purchased the occupancy of an existing run would find his improvements ready made; but these were of the usual kind. It was not a matter of colonial crudity. Most of the squatters had known a life ranging from the solid if plain comfort of the farm-house to the refinement of vicarage or manor-house. But the heavy cost of getting sheep and labour on to a station at all, and the insecurity of the squatter's tenure, postponed thoughts of civilized amenities in the bush.

What of his labourers? They are unsung heroes of the Squatting Age, and it does not detract from the determination and intelligence of the squatters to recall the service of their employees.

Most necessary and hardest to find were the shepherds. In the early days of squatting in the penal colonies they were convicts and ticket-of-leave men, and for some years after transportation had ceased, the majority of shepherds in the outer fringes of pastoral settlement were ex-convicts—'old lags'. They had a pride of profession, an *esprit de corps* supported by their own cant language, and they did not welcome free immigrant labourers into their company. 'Thank God,' an early writer reports one of them as saying, 'I'm not a bloody immigrant. Thank God I came out honourable. Some poor fellows are sent out for nothing, but thank God it was not for nothing I was sent out.'

They needed a firm hand and respected the man who was quick to see through them. Some squatters, so often much younger than their 'old-lag' servants, had much trouble with them. But experience of the bush in their earlier days of assignment had taught them its ways, and in general the squatters found them, once their respect had been gained, daring and hard working. It was they who transferred the flocks from Tasmania and New South Wales into Victoria, and from New South Wales into Queensland; and they were always to be found on the outer edge of settlement.

They were restless and fond of change, and, now being free to do so, moved from station to station, rarely staying more than a year at one place. Indeed, this mobility was characteristic of all free labour in Australia. The end of all a year's labour for £20 or £30 and rations was a complete and uninhibited spree at the nearest grog-shanty. As a class, the old-lag shepherds soon disappeared. Few of them married, and it was not many years before they died off, leaving no successors quite of their type.

Their place was taken by free immigrants; but immigrants were reluctant to take on the 'hatter's trade' of shepherding. It was regarded as a low-grade occupation—'crawling after sheep'—and it had the taint of convictism on it. In any case, immigrants coming from the sociableness of towns and villages in the old country feared the loneliness of the bush even more than they feared its dangers, the dangers of death by spear or thirst or snake-bite. And their conditions were always primitive, particularly on the out-stations.

So squatters were always short of shepherds and the flocks assigned to the care of any one shepherd continued to grow larger. On the whole it was either the less enterprising of free immigrants who took on shepherding, tremulous of its dangers but unable to discover an alternative; or it was the eccentrics or those people whose experience of life had made them avoid human society. One visitor to South Australia noted that within ten miles of his dwelling there were as shepherds and hut-keepers an apothecary, a lawyer's clerk, a counting-house clerk, three sailors, a tailor, a Portuguese sailor, a native of Ceylon, an Australian native, a barman, a gentleman's son brought up to no profession, a New Zealand merchant who had been burnt out, a second Portuguese who could understand no English, a lieutenant formerly in the service of the East India Company, and a gipsy.

For those who continued as shepherds for any length of time, their occupation made for eccentricity, even if they had not gone to it through an already acquired eccentricity. The shepherd's work was to take his flock out in the morning, preventing it from scattering too widely and keeping it on the move from time to time; and to bring it home at night. The flock was folded in hurdles and watched by a hut-keeper or anyone available, until dawn started the monotonous cycle once more.

It was a monotonous life, and, at least on the out-stations of a run, it was lonely. So it is natural that shepherds acquired the reputation of eccentricity. In part it was simply the dropping away of town conventions that had no use in the bush. But it was also the result of a lonely and monotonous life, exposed in new country to considerable danger, for it was mostly the isolated shepherds who were killed by the spears of aborigines or who lost their way and died of thirst.

So those who could choose were reluctant to go as shepherds. In 1842, when even unemployment was failing to drive urban workers up country, a writer in the *Sydney Herald* claimed that

even in the rare instances in which he is altogether shut out for weeks together from intercourse with his fellow-men, his social sympathies are awakened, and interested and amused by the animal creation. The feathered tenants of the grove—the kangaroo bounding across the plains—the opossum scaling the giant trees—the emu pacing with his majestic step— the black swan proudly sailing in the lake—the myriads of gay insects glittering in the air—the flocks committed to his pastoral charge, with the merry lambs frisking and gambolling all day long—and the very dog that crouches at his feet and licks his hand, and obeys his nod and beck—are the companions of his most sequestered hours, affording constant gratification to his eye, his ear and his imagination, and banishing that oppressive sense of solitude and abstraction which belongs to the inmate of the cell.

The labourers of Sydney remained unconvinced, and the scarcity of shepherds was a never-ending complaint.

A person of great importance to a station was the bullock-driver who, once a year, would take the bales of wool to the port and return with the year's supplies. The journey was slow and the bullock-driver from a remote station might be months on the road, with his bullocks his only companions for much of that time. The bullock-driver gained a reputation for eloquence to bullocks and taciturnity towards his fellow-men. Hood, indeed, doubted his humanity. 'The bullock-driver,' he wrote, 'is a being completely *sui generis*; he is the most cruel and profane wretch that breathes; his cruelty and drunkenness render him more a brute than the animal he tortures.' But, their roughness of manner granted, they were persons of trust and were generally found worthy of it.

Once a year, also, arrived the shearers. They were always the object of complaint for the roughness of their work and the insolence of their behaviour; and many a squatter was left to finish his shearing for himself with what help he could muster from his own men.

There were many other classes of bush-workers, such as stockmen of the cattle-stations, daring riders and scornful of the shepherds who in those days were not mounted, and the migratory bush mechanics—carpenters, blacksmiths, masons, sawyers, splitters, and fencers. The bush mechanics became more numerous and more important in the squatting areas as the early phase of crude occupation gave way to improvement. By that time, free immigration had diluted the old-lag element, and diggers were turning from the goldfields to find more enduring employment in the bush. Then the character of bush-workers changed for the better and they proved both more dependable and more independent.

Such in general were the labourers who were the rank and file of that pastoral army which tamed the interior. The squatter and his men might best hope for an uneventful life, for any event worthy of notice was likely to be unpleasant—the spread of scab in the flocks, a bush fire, a drought or a flood, robbery under arms by bush-rangers or attack by aborigines.

The relations of the squatters and the aborigines have not yet been satisfactorily studied. It is clear that two cultures were meeting which could not both survive; and, however defenceless a lonely shepherd's hut might seem, power was in the end on the shepherd's side. If white men shot the kangaroos, it was natural that aborigines who did not know any deed of surrender of the tribal lands should turn to the squatter's sheep. It is probable, too, that the interference of shepherds with native women caused much of the trouble; and, on the other hand, the station stores were always a temptation to the natives.

A cause of trouble as yet little studied was probably the white man's unwitting desecration of sacred places associated with the totemic ancestors. Many of the attacks on the whites seemed to come out of a blue sky and to be ascribable only to innate treachery in the aborigines. Such attacks may well have had causes that the white men could have understood only if they had gained an intimate knowledge of aboriginal lore. The relations of both races were often friendly, but in general they make a sad story. There were killings on both sides, and the white man killed less by musket-shot than by his diseases and by his unknowing destruction of that aboriginal culture which had given the natives cohesion and the will to live.

There were well-meaning attempts in the 'forties to protect the natives. The Port Phillip Protectorates, 1838–50, failed miserably, although not from want of will, for they had no adequate basis in knowledge of aboriginal life. Nor, indeed, could anything have saved traditional food sources and traditional tribal movements, cere-monials and relationships from destruction short of reservation of the country on a vast scale for the aborigines, and the squatting expansion made such a policy unlikely. Meanwhile, to the squatters and their men on the outer fringes of settlement, the aborigines appeared largely, although not exclusively, as one of the dangers of pioneering, and were often treated accordingly.

This chapter began with a contrast between the finished perfection of Camden Park and the crude improvisation of squatting in new country. Yet the squatters were in large part drawn from the classes of society in the old country to whom the leisured comfort of Camden might seem the natural end of their endeavours. And in all the rough pioneering labour of the earliest stage of squatting, they did not lose the assumptions of a leisured class. It was a case of postponement rather than renunciation of that life.

Yet the squatter, though he might be but recently come from

England, seemed to the visitor typically Australian, as, shaded by a cabbage-tree hat and disguised by a luxuriant growth of beard and moustache, he rode into Melbourne, scattering the dust or mud of its streets from his horse's hooves and jumping the gutter chasms that recalled the newness of the town's foundation.

The distinctiveness of appearance might be superficial; but in truth a fundamental change was taking place in many of them. Though they might bring the inherited assumptions of the old world, they fell, in many cases, under the spell of the new. So Alfred Joyce wrote home to explain why he had no intention of returning to his native land. 'I have become so accustomed to this colony that I should not be happy anywhere else. The prospect of English winters and long gloomy weather would frighten me from going there. I am too used now to sunshine to be able to be satisfied long without it.'

The letters of John Cotton of Doogalook on the Goulburn are full of appreciative references to the birds and flowers and the natural scenery of the country; and are accompanied by the most beautiful drawings of all these things. For he was both a naturalist and an artist—a point that may remind us that the majority of squatters were fair representatives of the English middle-class culture of their times. Even the first dray-load would contain a selection of books.

The example of John Cotton may introduce a further stage, for the phase of temporary makeshift began to give way to more enduring improvements during the 'forties and 'fifties, except in areas only then being brought into use. Cotton arrived in Melbourne in 1843 and bought a right of station on the Goulburn from its previous occupant. 'There is upon the station', he wrote, 'a four-roomed slab house . . . but as the house is not large enough to hold my family, I am now building a slab house of larger dimensions of sawn wood.'

That sentence marks a new phase of development in the social history of squatting—the family phase. Both at master and servant level, for it was the time of assisted female immigration and of Caroline Chisholm's labours in family colonization, this did much to transform the old untidiness of temporary improvisation. The untidiness of the Australian countryside did not give way at once to a trim English neatness; it has not done so yet. But the squatters began to build more substantial houses and to plant gardens, to afford, in short, more of the amenities of life.

A more substantial house implied that the squatter had overtaken his first outlay of capital; it generally implied that he was bringing a wife to the bush and so transforming its social life; and it indicated some improvement in his tenure of his run or of part of it, particularly after new land regulations in 1848 had granted leases of up to four-teen years in certain areas with compensation for improvements and the right of pre-emption. The solid stone or brick homesteads of such areas as the western district of Victoria belong for the most part to the 'sixties and 'seventies; but even in the 'forties and 'fifties sub-stantial building in stone was beginning.

Part of this phase of development which brought a radical change into pastoral life was the fencing of runs. This also depended on improved security of tenure, but it was the labour shortage during the gold rushes which replaced shepherds and sheep folds by large fenced paddocks and boundary riders. Their shepherds deserting to the gold-fields, squatters found that sheep suffered no harm from wandering at will. Ceaseless war had reduced the dingo menace, and both sheep and fleece benefited when the nightly crowding into sheep-folds was abandoned. Despite the initial cost of fencing, the result was economy, for one or two boundary riders replaced six or more shepherds and hut-keepers, while the carrying capacity of a given area was considerably increased.

Fencing was an economic measure; but the spirit of the building of houses and planting of gardens may be seen in a letter written home by Alfred Joyce in 1858:

I intend building a two-storey house next, as it is very flat all around our place, and we are not able to get much view from the ground. I am going to pay a little attention to the ornamental with respect to the house and garden. Hitherto we have studied the useful only, but I think the time has arrived when we may look to blend some of the ornamental with it. As it is probable that I and my family are likely to remain at Norwood for many years yet, it is as well to render it a home consistent with our means.

The useful that he had studied hitherto had been a native Australian product; the ornamental was imported European tradition. The result of their blending was something not quite European. There were nostalgic importations of all sorts, English or Scottish styles of domestic architecture, English trees and flowers, the rabbit and the fox for the huntsman. Wealthier families might enforce their attach-ment to the old world by sending their sons to Oxford and their daughters to finishing schools in London or Paris.

Nevertheless, the life of the station, even when pioneering days were over, had taken on a recognizably Australian character. The European house was surrounded by wide Australian verandas. Its approach was as likely to be through an avenue of gum-trees as through an avenue of imported pines or populars. Even the squatter's sports took on a new air. His shooting was not governed by traditional rules, and the exhibitions of horse-breaking and the picnic races which brought families together from miles around, and the barn dances which followed them, allowed an informality and a social mixing that did not mark the hunt and the hunt ball of the squatter's former home.

The transformation went deeper. That ideal of a life of leisured enjoyment which Wakefield had painted in his *Letter from Sydney* did not take firm root. Long after the pioneering days, the squatter remained a worker on his run as well as its manager, just as his wife found herself faced with more tasks in the household than she might have expected at home. A symbol of this on the average run was the early telescoping, dictated by the working day and shortage of domestic labour, of tea and dinner into a meal at sundown rightly named, after its main beverage, tea.

The result was to narrow somewhat the social difference between the squatter and the smaller people of both town and country. That did not prevent bitter dispute; but it was not dispute between people of entirely different worlds.

The point is of some importance, for the squatters at this time were becoming a political group, aggrieved by the British Government's land policy on the one hand, challenged by a new democracy on the other. Their association in political action was in large part made and led by men of old-established colonial families, such as James Macarthur, son of the great John, and William Charles Wentworth. For the newly arrived squatter was too fully occupied on his run and too seldom in the town to take more than an intermittent part in political agitation. The role of the older landed families was to give continuity and organization to the landed interest as a whole.

It is probably for this reason that the squatters never gained the overwhelming political influence in the newly settled Port Phillip District which they gained in the 'central district' of New South Wales; for Port Phillip had no families of locally inherited wealth and prestige, and its political life early on took on a flavour as much urban and mercantile as pastoralist.

But New South Wales proper had its traditional leaders in public affairs, who could express the common grievances and common demands of the squatters. Both grievances and demands turned in the main on the land question.

Free land grants had been finally abandoned in 1831, and, under Wakefieldian influence, the price at which crown land was sold was raised by successive stages until in 1842 the minimum upset price was fixed at £1 per acre in all the Australian colonies. Meanwhile, the squatters had been allowed to trespass at a small fee; but merely as holders of a temporary right to graze their stock on the waste lands of the Crown, who could be displaced by would-be buyers, without compensation for improvements and without right of pre-emption. It was found in practice that the high price of £1 per acre did give them virtual security, for in most areas that price could not attract buyers; but this result was both unintended and not immediately recognized.

The squatters for their part had mixed their hard labour and considerable capital with the land, and believed that they had a moral right to it. What they wanted, in effect, was a perpetual tenure at a much lower price.

British governments, with an eye to the needs of future generations, were not prepared to alienate in perpetuity vast areas of land to a few people. Governor Gipps (1838–46), who saw the elements of justice in the claims of both sides, tried, in two sets of proposals published in 1844, to reconcile the reasonable ambitions of present occupants of pastoral lands with the interests of future generations. It was unfortunate that proposals which were, on the whole, eminently fair, nevertheless contained a sufficient element of doubt and difficulty to make the genuine squatter responsive to an opposition organized in large part by the absentee capitalists of the pastoral expansion. The occupation proposals brought no threat to the squatter working his own run. They attempted to define the normal run held by pastoral licence as an area not exceeding twenty square miles or capable of carrying more than 4,000 sheep or 500 cattle. Those who occupied more would have to surrender the surplus or take out additional licences. As the licences merely gave temporary permission to graze on Crown lands, it was reasonable to restrict occupants to areas adequate for the stock they owned or might hope to own in the near future. The occupation regulations by themselves would not have disturbed resident squatters and might indeed have helped to give them access to lands which were held under licence by people who could not stock them adequately. A capitalist such as Benjamin Boyd, however, might have had to take out sixty or more additional licences.

At £10 per annum for the licence, even this was not a major blow, although men who had got themselves into debt in a time of depression might feel it to be so. But the occupation proposals were tied to proposals for progressive purchase, which were the main bone of contention. By this plan every squatter under licence should be given an opportunity of buying 320 acres of his run as a homestead at the end of five years, the purchase securing his right to hold the whole run under licence for the next eight years. At the end of this period he should again have the opportunity to purchase not less than 320 acres with a further security of tenure of the whole run for eight years. If purchase had been at the minimum upset price of £1 an acre, this, after the first five years of occupation would have amounted to an annual payment of £40 in addition to the licence fee.

But sale had to be by public auction, and the squatter in possession might conceivably find himself outbid by someone ready to pay a high price for 320 acres in order to get occupation of a developed run. The credit allowed for the squatter's improvements gave him an advantage, but not absolute security. It was this uncertainty which made the genuine squatter responsive to the initial agitation against Gipps's proposals. To men who were fighting against heavy burdens of debt in a time of depressed prices, and conscious of having borne the brunt of battle against fire and flood on their holdings, scab and catarrh in their flocks, even moderate imposts could seem the last impossible straw. But time and improving prices could have taken the edge off this response if certainty of tenure had been secured to them, and indeed the prospect of security did so in the later stages of the controversy.

The Boyds and the Wentworths, holders of vast pastoral empires, had far more to lose. As Mr K. Buckley has shown,[1] Boyd might have had to pay £20,000 or more every eight years, and Wentworth over £6,000. The Legislative Council of New South Wales, the stronghold of such men, provided sixteen of the leaders of the Pastoral Association formed to fight the regulations; and all the members of the Council's Committee on Crown land grievances were members of this Association. Nevertheless, Gipps's readiness to meet the difficulties of genuine squatters was winning a degree of success for the intention of his proposals when a change of government removed Lord Stanley from the Colonial Office and with him Gipps's support. Eventually the squatters gained a large degree of security by a Waste Lands Act of 1846 which, as interpreted by an Order in Council of 1847, allowed the outback squatter a lease of fourteen years with a right of pre-emption and compensation for improvements. The agitation did not wholly die, for the Order in Council was permissive and was not applied to all areas.

Long unable to get its way from the British Government, the landed interest had taken to itself an agitation for self-government which previously had been the personal interest of colonial patriots like Wentworth rather than a widely and deeply felt issue. Some

[1] See his two articles in *Historical Studies, Australia and New Zealand* on 'Gipps and the Graziers of N.S.W., 1841–6', vol. 6, 24 May 1955, and vol. 7, 26 May 1956.

concession was made to this agitation by an imperial act of 1842 which provided that two-thirds of the members of the Legislative Council of New South Wales should be elected by the colonists. But the disposal of the waste lands was still reserved to the Crown; for the British Government continued to regard the disposal of the waste lands of the empire as an imperial trust.

So the agitation for self-government continued, and was not fully satisfied by the Australian Colonies Government Act of 1850. This Act separated Port Phillip from New South Wales as the Colony of Victoria and thereby answered a vigorous campaign in that area for separation. It proposed to extend to all the other colonies the system of partly elected councils already established in New South Wales. And it allowed the colonial legislative councils a limited right to alter their own constitutions. But it still reserved the control of waste lands to the Crown and did not yet hold out any promise of fully responsible government in colonial affairs.

The discovery of gold in 1851 altered the case, and in 1852 dispatches from Pakington and Newcastle informed the colonists that they could draft constitutions giving them practically all they wanted, including control over the disposal of Crown lands.

The Legislative Council of New South Wales had needed no further invitation than the Act of 1850 to set to work, under Wentworth's guidance, on the task of constitution making. That council most fully represented the squatters, and it was clear that its draft of a constitution would recognize the claims of landed property to political authority.

The right of the landed interest to lead was asserted the more vigorously because it was being challenged. For there was also in the 'forties a political agitation of more radical hue, fed by the free immigration of that time. The smaller people, from labourers and artisans to shopkeepers, could find leaders in men of independent mind like Robert Lowe and the fiery Scots Minister, John Dunmore Lang; and they found, for a time, allies in the merchant classes of the city who were not yet fully admitted to partnership by the colonial gentry.

Faced by their discountenancing of the squatters' claim to power, Wentworth made the classic statement of that claim in a defiant speech to the electors of Sydney in 1851:

If it had not been for the squatting class, when transportation was discontinued to the colony, it must have dwindled into insignificance, they would have had the grass now growing in their streets; if it had not been for this class their magnificent city would have shrunk into a small fishing town, unfamed, and disregarded by European nations. Their 60,000 inhabitants, if it had not been for this class, would not have exceeded one-third of that number. It was to this class that they were indebted for the tall ships within their harbour. It was this class that had caused the lofty warehouses to rise on their quays; it was this class that provided the splendid equipages that rolled through their streets, and afforded the means for all those appliances of wealth and splendour which abounded in their dwellings. It was to him and to his class that they owed these things—it was to this much-abused class that they were indebted for all their greatness, all the comforts, all the luxuries, that they possessed.

The answer was given without restraint of language on many a radical platform and in many a radical newspaper; but perhaps it may be more typically represented by the old bush ballad, 'The Squatter of the Olden Time,' for it expresses a vein of scepticism towards the pretensions of colonial wealth which has been a recurrent motif of Australian democracy:

I'll sing to you a fine new song, made by my blessed mate,
Of a fine Australian squatter who had a fine estate,
Who swore by right pre-emptive at a sanguinary rate
That by his rams, his ewes, his lambs, Australia was made great—
    Like a fine Australian squatter, one of the olden time.

His hut around was hung with guns, whips, spurs, and boots and shoes,
And kettles and tin pannikins to hold the tea he brews;
And here his worship lolls at ease and takes his smoke and snooze,
And quaffs his cup of hysonskin, the beverage old chums choose—
    Like a fine Australian squatter, one of the olden time.

And when shearing time approaches he opens hut to all,
And though ten thousand are his flocks, he featly shears them all,
Even to the scabby wanderer you'd think no good at all;
For while he fattens all the great, he boils down all the small—
    Like a fine old Murray squatter, one of the olden time.

And when his worship comes to town his agents for to see,
His wool to ship, his beasts to sell, he lives right merrily;
The club his place of residence, as becomes a bush J.P.,
He darkly hints that Thompson's run from scab is scarcely free—
    This fine old Murray settler, one of the olden time.

And now his fortune he has made to England straight goes he,
But finds with grief he's not received as he had hoped to be.
His friends declare his habits queer, his language much too free,
And are somewhat apt to cross the street when him they chance to see—
    This fine old Australian squatter, the boy of the olden time.

In short, the stage was set for a struggle between two conceptions of what colonial societies should be like, between the rule of a landed gentry and an aggressive democracy.

7

GOLD AND DEMOCRACY

Australian history in the colonial period has every appearance of class conflict. Harshest division of all, the early gulf between gaoler and gaoled bred the miasma of prejudice which divided the penal colonies into the two camps of emancipists and exclusives. Their hostilities faded with the ending of the convict system, but gave way to division between wealthy masters, whatever their origins, and the labouring classes; and the gulf between them was but slenderly bridged before the gold-rushes of the 'fifties by the tiny middle group of farmers, retailers and independent artisans. Even when the gold-rushes had done much to fill that middle gap, the loud-voiced struggles between democratic lower houses and propertied upper houses seemed to continue the theme of bitter and militant class conflict.

Yet the impression of many contemporary observers was quite different, at least during and after the gold-rushes. They were struck by the absence of the entrenched social divisions of the old world. They noticed a spirit of equality and independence and ascribed it to a wide distribution of a fair livelihood and of opportunity for betterment.

So George Higinbotham, liberal editor of the Melbourne *Argus*, claimed in 1856 that manhood suffrage would bring no threat to property in Victoria. 'The fear of attack on property is warranted in old countries where a dangerous class, hating the wealthy, has sprung up, as pauperism grew concomitantly with wealth. We have hardly any paupers and no dangerous class.'

Some reconciliation of the conflict between the two impressions of class struggle and social fluidity must be sought.

A good deal of the more militant and theoretical radicalism of early colonial days was a product of the old world rather than of the

new. The feelings of immigrants newly come from the political
ferment of English chartism, Irish revolt and continental revolution
might be kept alive for a time by colonial conditions such as the
depression of the 'forties and the arrogance of police on the gold-
fields of the 'fifties. But there were other and more enduring conditions
which tempered such feelings.

Irish and European rebels found in the colonies no such oppression
as they had known at home. Their old hatreds could fade into a mere
suspicion of authority. Moreover, the colonial social hierarchy
lacked the appearance of permanence that marked the old world. It
carried no sanction of long and inherited custom, and change of
status was a familiar colonial experience even before the rapid
changes of fortune that marked the years of the gold discoveries.
Therefore, social divisions were neither accepted as an inevitable
part of the social order nor regarded as something which could be
altered only by a radical subversion of the whole.

The impression of social fluidity, which was created by the rise of
individuals from obscurity to moderate comfort and even to wealth,
was not weakened by the fact that the great majority continued to
depend on the sale of their labour to employers; for statistical
generalizations are less obvious than individual cases.

As imported radicalism was modified by colonial conditions, a
distinctively Australian democracy was born. It was sceptical of the
pretensions of wealth and militant in tone; but it was compromising in
practice and concerned with the particular rather than the general.
Its growth is the main theme of the remaining chapters of this book.

The beginnings of this colonial democracy can be seen even before
the gold-rushes; but it was in the 'fifties that its main outlines were
clearly drawn. Then, to the accompaniment of the gold-rushes,
colonial legislative councils were drafting the new constitutions
which the dispatches from Pakington and Newcastle had invited.
With these constitutions, there set in one of the most vigorous
periods of political discussion in Australian history.

In the course of this prolonged debate, opposing groups justified
their conflicting proposals by much searching into political theory.
It was, indeed, the most fertile period in Australian political thinking
before federation; for the political temper of the Australian community had not yet been determined and the question at stake was
no less than this: Who should have the shaping of the community in
their hands and what should that shape be?

If it seemed inevitable at first that the pastoralists would have that
power, and that they would use it to mould a community in their
own image, we must remember how uncertain their political tenure,

like the tenure of their lands, was. The inrush of new numbers set against the background of the vigorous if spasmodic radical agitation of the 'forties might well seem to Wentworth and his fellows to threaten them with 'a radical democracy'.

The issue depended, no doubt, less on victory in argument than on the changes then taking place in the distribution of wealth and in the social composition of the colonies. The point was not immediately obvious, and while the evident threat added an edge and a vigour to the debate, Wentworth and his associates of the New South Wales Legislative Council drafted their constitutional proposals in the belief that wise legislation might erect enduring barriers against the ill-humours of the people.

In the constitution drafted in 1853 by a committee of the council under Wentworth's direction, these barriers were of three types. The first was a nominated upper house to check any tendency to rash democracy in the lower. Wentworth had gone further, to propose an hereditary colonial peerage; this was laughed out of court as 'a bunyip aristocracy', and Wentworth himself did not press it. The second barrier was a distribution of electorates to give rural districts and landowners a greater proportion of representation than the town. The third consisted of measures to make amendment difficult, for Wentworth's draft required two-thirds majorities for major amendments.

A further barrier was the restriction of the right to vote for the lower house to people able to satisfy certain property qualifications; but these were not high and it was clear that Wentworth looked to other measures than a restricted franchise to provide that security for person and property, law and order, to which he appealed in justifying his proposals.

The strongest defence against democracy was the obstacles opposed to amendment. They were in effect overthrown by the Imperial Parliament's Act of 1855 which enabled the queen to give the royal assent to the colonial constitution; for that Act allowed the colonists to amend the constitution itself by ordinary bill and so to eliminate the requirement of two-thirds majorities contained in it.

The Legislative Councils of Victoria, South Australia and Tasmania drafted constitutions that were in many respects similar; but all three provided for upper houses that should be elected by professional people and the holders of high property qualifications. It was a mark of South Australia's more evenly balanced society that it provided manhood suffrage for the lower house in its original constitution.

Wentworth's proposal for a colonial House of Lords provides a

key to the squatters' imagination of what Australia should be like.
From first to last, as Professor A. C. V. Melbourne showed in his
William Charles Wentworth, the consistency that runs through
Wentworth's inconsistencies is this dream of a colonial gentry of
landed families leading the colonies in politics as in wealth and
culture. It was an idea already tottering in the England of the
Great Exhibition of 1851; but the pedigree of the political ideas of
pastoral conservatives in the New South Wales of that time is to be
found in the eighteenth century, the age of Burke, rather than the
nineteenth.

Their assumptions could last the longer because the pre-eminence
of the pastoral industry and the smallness of the colonial middle
class had made the pastoralists leaders in fact as well as in claim.
There had been no industrial revolution in the colonies, and they
were separated by 12,000 miles of sea from the new liberal doctrines
of industrial England. Indeed, it was more than the oceans, it was a
generation which divided the landed interest from their liberal
opponents of the town of Sydney.

As he saw the colony being changed by immigration and the
assertive claims of new classes, the old battler—for battler Wentworth always was, whether for good or ill causes—saw his vision
crumbling. He had led the colony to self-government, only to see
that government threatened by a democracy which, in his view,
would destroy any social order worth striving for. There is no room
here for men of wealth, he complained. What can they aspire to? 'I
will tell the council: they aspire to a speedy migration to other lands
. . . where the democratic and levelling principles so rapidly increasing
here are scouted. . . . Who would stay here if he could avoid it? Who
with ample means would ever return?'

Wentworth did in fact spend most of his remaining years in
England after 1853; yet he had been the most ardent patriot in the
public life of the colony, and he had been its stoutest fighter for those
freedoms it possessed—freedom of the press, trial by jury and colonial
self-government. But he and his fellow drafters of the new constitution believed that it should first and foremost safeguard property.
Inevitably they distrusted theory, for theory took the form of appeal
to abstract reason and the natural rights of men; it was a French
revolutionary sort of thing, they felt, out of relation with practical
facts and productive only of discontent and disorder. All social
order rested on property, and the end of government must be to
preserve property and the ordered society that went with it.

A landed generation that read Burke and looked at the French
Revolution from its latter end of disorder, tyranny and war had its

D

views confirmed by the revolutions of 1848, when, as James Macarthur put it in a speech on Wentworth's constitution, 'the Continent
of Europe was rocked to its foundations by the prevailing genius of
democracy—when the floodgates of anarchy were unclosed, and the
landmarks of civilization in danger of being overwhelmed by the
devastating torrent'.

They did not feel that their assumptions required further supporting argument. Yet argument, and theoretical argument at that,
could not be avoided; for the makers of constitutions were obliged
to justify them and to defend them against vigorous opposition. But
the distrust of theory pervaded even their theorizing; their arguments
were pragmatic and empirical. 'Shall we quit the safe and beaten
path of constitutional precedent', asked James Macarthur in that
same speech, 'to follow in the train of those who covet power for
their own ends, or who would risk all in the visionary hope of
perfection?' There were many variants of the familiar argument that
the wisdom of the past lives on in its legacy to the present, and that
unless things have clearly fallen into disorder, their existence is a
presumption in their favour against abstract notions of what ought
to be.

Rights were not the original condition of man, but the product of
ordered society; and ordered society depended on the leadership of
its wisest, in short its propertied, part. 'The right to elect representatives', declared James Martin, the attorney-general, when manhood
suffrage was being debated in New South Wales in 1858, 'is no
original right of man, because it is a thing unknown to man, except
in civil society.' The franchise was a mere matter of expediency and
the house should adopt a franchise 'not in accordance with the wild
and extravagant theories of ill-informed and unreflecting demagogues
of the hour, but with a view to the grand ends for which any franchise
whatever is given; among the most important of those ends must be
ranked the necessity of imposing a strong check upon the arbitrary
will of the multitude'.

A Victorian conservative paper, *Australia Felix,* conceded that
the physical and moral well-being of every individual had an equal
claim to consideration, but that consideration would not come from
'the vacillating multitude' subjected 'to the sway of a few master
spirits—who will make use of eloquence and impudence to bind the
many, even with the chains of their own passions. . . . Independence
is not for man, and "the sovereign will of the people" is a dream of
the imagination'.

Radicals claimed that parliament should represent 'the people',
and there was much discussion of this term. The conservative argu-

ment was in general that as reason should rule and control the passions, so the mob should be controlled by the smaller and wiser part of the people. Political wisdom was not to 'be measured out by the square yard at the corners of the streets'. 'If the representation of the country', declared Stuart Alexander Donaldson in the New South Wales debate on manhood suffrage, 'depended upon bare numbers, the elections would be decided by the most unthinking, unreflecting—the most influenced by partisans—by demagogues; who would cheer without hearing, and shout without knowing what they were shouting for.' In the same debate and the same mood, Martin claimed to take 'the voice of the people . . . not from the large mass of stupidity which degrades, but the smaller portion which ennobles it'.

So Wentworth addressed an election appeal to 'the rational, the sensible, the calm, the orderly men of Sydney—the educated and propertied classes'; and told a hostile crowd:

> Whether you elect me or not is to me personally a matter of no consequence, but it may be a matter of importance to you and to the public. . . . If it appears that the alteration of the franchise shall overpower the education and respectability of the city, and I am rejected—one of two questions will be decided, either I am not deserving of the constituency, or this constituency is not worthy of me. This question cannot be answered by men whose interests and passions are inflamed. It must be referred to a remote tribunal, where all the events and circumstances attending it will be calmly weighed. It must be referred to the tribunal of posterity, and to that tribunal I fear not to appeal. [He agreed, he said] with that ancient and venerable constitution that treated those who had no property as infants, or idiots, unfit to have any voice in the management of the State.

Wentworth felt little need to argue this view of the 'insensate populace',

> The brute crowd whose envious zeal
> Huzzas each turn of fortune's wheel;
> And loudest shouts, when lowest lie,
> Exalted worth and station high.

But it was rationalized by Sir Alfred Stephen in the discussion on manhood suffrage; 'the general rule is unquestionable, that the most intelligent and upright are those who possess or have acquired property; that ordinarily the poorest in a community, from causes often beyond their control, are both uneducated and ignorant; and that men are prone to crime in proportion to their ignorance'.

Such an argument could lend an added sanction to the representation of property rather than numbers; and there was a preference for landed property which reflected the existing but passing state of affairs and a fear of 'the democratic influence of our overgrown metropolis'. The squatting interest, claimed Wentworth, was the prominent interest of the colony and must be so for ages to come, for to no other cultivation could 'the illimitable wilds of the interior' be applied. It was four times as valuable to the colony as gold and would be on the increase when that, he hoped, would decline.

As to Sydney, which with a third of the colony's population returned only three members out of thirty-two, the merchants were unproductive and there was 'no urgent necessity' for them. Henry Parkes's moderately radical newspaper, *The Empire*, quoted with delight the comment of the London *Times*: 'One might imagine that it was some courtier of Charles I declaiming against the refractory city of London, or some sanguine Jacobite exulting over the time when he might trample out the spirit of commerce, and, with it, of freedom'.

The arguments of Wentworth and his fellows were the political manifestation of their ideal of a society resting on its pastoral industry and led by an aristocracy of landowners. That ideal was painted in darker colours by their opponents. If it were in the power of the squatting class, declared *The Empire*,

to continue to hold the country as a sheep-walk, it might be considered to have attained the maximum of its material prosperity. . . . The eternal bullock-dray dragging its slow length along a rugged road through a cheerless tenantless wilderness would be quite in keeping with isolated serfs, living or rather existing in bark huts on salt beef and damper, in the interior. Ours would be a country without hope—a people living without God in the world. . . . Australia would be doomed to witness the reproduction under her sunny skies of the most repulsive features of the social system of the Dark Ages, aggravated by an atheism grafted upon ignorance in the masses, and a worse than Irish absenteeism on the part of her Shepherd Kings. A few hundreds of Australian magnates, in the receipt of princely incomes, might shine in the fashionable circles of London. But such would be the scope and summit, the nature and extent of a national splendour that might be fitly compared with the gaseous coruscation emanating from a grave.

The lower part of the people, in short, did not accept with meekness the descriptions of its weakness of head and strength of passion; and the latter quality at least is evident in much of the uninhibited newspaper invective of the time. Wentworth's constitution, declared the *People's Advocate*, was a bastard offspring of tyranny, under the guise of liberty; a nauseous fungus rudely plucked from an old stump, and forcibly tried to be engrafted on the stem of a young sapling; upon which the experiments of quacks have failed, and which is now left to the tender mercies of wretches, whose loftiest aspirations never reached the zenith of mediocrity; whose honesty in politics found an only parallel in their morals.

There was argument, however, as well as abuse directed against 'the wool-growing oligarchs', and argument which came from more than one section of the community. The most obvious argument was that people were more important than interests. So the Scots minister, John Dunmore Lang, a doughty if sometimes wrong-headed fighter for freedom, described the distribution of electorates in Wentworth's constitution as 'of the most barefaced, impudent, iniquitous description imaginable—a system of representation under which nearly one half of the population had only one-sixth part of the representative assigned to it, while the other half had five-sixths'.

Though he claimed that numerically equal electorates would represent both property and numbers fairly, he shared the common radical view that those whom the shoe pinched should have the right to complain, and that the resort to talk of the virtue and wisdom of the propertied people simply concealed selfish and ulterior motives. Almost every provision the proposed constitution contained, declared Rober Lowe, 'was made subordinate to the ulterior object of obtaining for certain colonists the absolute possession and ownership of enormous tracts of the public lands'. Indeed, it is clear that hostility to the squatter constitutions went far beyond a debate on political machinery. What was feared was that the pastoralists would use their political power, control of Crown lands being surrendered to colonial parliaments, to entrench themselves in economic as well as in political privilege. The fierce opposition to the granting of long-term leases to squatters in Victoria is one symptom of the common fear.

Temporary alliances of merchants and manufacturers with urban radicals against the pastoralists could not alter the fact that colonial democrats were quick to be suspicious of the pretensions of property, however gained.

Stephen's argument that wisdom went with the possession of property was disputed as doubtful in itself and particularly doubtful in the colonies. Worth and talent might be found outside the ranks of property, so often discreditably gained. When it was proposed to make the possession of property worth £10,000 a qualification for membership of the Victorian Upper House, Fawkner commented, 'The Upper House will be filled with publicans; that is quite clear'.

Indeed, this scepticism of the claims of wealth has been a recurrent theme in Australian political controversy, for colonial wealth rarely carried with it the sanction of inherited custom. Higinbotham referred to the classes from which the Victorian Upper House was drawn as 'the wealthy lower orders' and H. J. Wrixon wrote in his *Democracy in Australia* (1868), 'Wealth is the only badge of our aristocracy, but it confers a nobility neither exclusive nor enduring'.

Colonial cynicism found its readiest expression in the bush ballads, as in these stanzas from 'Sam Holt':

> Oh! don't you remember the cattle you duffed,
>   And your luck at the Sandy Creek rush,
> And the poker you played, and the bluffs that you bluffed,
>   And your habits of holding a flush?

> And don't you remember the pasting you got
>   By the boys down in Callaghan's store,
> When Tim Hooligan found a fifth ace in his hand,
>   And you holding his pile upon four?

> You were not the cleanest potato, Sam Holt,
>   You had not the cleanest of fins,
> But you made your pile on the Towers, Sam Holt,
>   And that covers the most of your sins.

> They say you've ten thousand per annum, Sam Holt,
>   In England, a park and a drag;
> Perhaps you forget you were six months ago
>   In Queensland a-humping your swag.

The arguments so far mentioned in opposition to the squatter constitutions were of two sorts: those which played on the theme, 'A man's a man for a' that', and those which doubted whether colonial men of property held any monopoly of political virtue and wisdom. But there was another form of argument that was historically important. Pastoral conservatives had asserted the claims of landed property. 'But was there no other property', asked one man, no longer a radical, '—no shipping, banking, or other interest equally entitled with the squatting to a share in the representation?'

There was, indeed, at this time and for some few years to come, an alliance of city merchants with the radicals against the assumed right of the landowning classes to continuing leadership. This was a response to the favour shown to the latter in the political arrangements of the 'forties and again in Wentworth's new constitution.

Lang was sceptical. 'We have just as little to expect in the way of

liberal and enlightened government for the colony from our mercantile aristocracy as we have from the squattocracy itself.' Nevertheless,
this alliance had practical results. It made for a tempering of extreme
radical demands and it gave the democrats the support of powerful
city interests in their struggle to gain political rights from their
landowning opponents. The alliance was the more easily formed
because the main strength of colonial radicalism at this time rested,
so it seems, less in the ranks of unskilled labour than in the small
middle-class people ranging from skilled artisans to journalists,
shopkeepers and petty manufacturers.

So we may understand the combination of militancy of tone with
compromise in action. Argument is conducted with a heat and personal invective which modern libel laws would not allow; but there
is no demand to turn society upside down, no demand to eliminate
any class, only a demand for a more equal or wider sharing of
society's privileges. And that was something very flexible which
could readily ally itself for a time with a moneyed group, the city
merchants, whose views were less radical than rival to those of the
landowners.

Henry Parkes, for example, who received his earliest political
education in English chartism and was now leading the colonial
opposition to Wentworth's constitution, never tired of the theme
that social classes had duties towards each other, including the duty
of the employee to his employer; and for him one of the main ends
of popular education was to teach a sense of mutual duties. He is a
typical example of this militant but compromising radicalism.

He described Wentworth's constitution as 'a monstrous production' of a 'mongrel body', and the squatters as 'the most useless men
in the council'. But when Wentworth 'honoured him with the title
of arch-anarchist', he denied any belief in republican government.
He did not want a 'Yankee constitution' any more than Wentworth.
'But by all that was sacred, by the God who had given them a great
and powerful country to dwell in, he for one would never consent
to have a Norfolk Island constitution.'

It was the quality of this radicalism that it could win sufficient
support outside its own ranks to turn the scale. The new constitutions
were introduced in the four colonies of New South Wales, Victoria,
Tasmania,[1] and South Australia in 1855–6. Within a very few years,
all of them had been amended in a democratic direction. There were
checks on too hasty democracy still, by way of unequal electorates
and propertied upper houses; but by 1858 all had gained vote by
ballot and all but Tasmania had gained manhood suffrage, while

[1] This name officially replaced Van Diemen's Land in the Constitution of 1856.

Wentworth's bar to change, the two-thirds majorities, had been amended out of the constitution of New South Wales.

These changes took place at the height of the gold-rushes, in a decade which increased Victoria's population from 77,000 to 541,000 and that of all the Australian colonies from 438,000 to 1,168,000

Historians have warned against a temptation to find in these gold-rushes the cause of developments which would have happened, if more slowly, without them. Merchants, shop-keepers and artisans would have fought the squatters' monopoly in any case, and would in time have won their victories for 'democracy'. But one finds this view more actively expressed by historians outside Victoria. New South Wales was an old established colony able to absorb its relatively minor gold-rush as a colourful but not cataclysmic chapter in its history; infant Victoria could not do so. In ten years it was transformed from a pastoral extension of Tasmania and New South Wales into a bustling, aggressively self-assertive colony of over half a million people, close on 140,000 of them living in Melbourne, which was already on the way to becoming a metropolis.

This was a change in numbers; it was also a change in kind. The change in numbers was important. In the years 1853–60 which saw a drop of 76,000 in average annual emigration from the British Isles, there was a rise from 26,000 to 46,000 in average annual immigration into the Australian and New Zealand colonies. It was gold which gave these normally less attractive colonies of the South Seas a positive increase of immigrants at a time when emigration in general was falling away. If golden Victoria got the lion's share, the prosperity which the Victorian market brought to its neighbouring colonies made them attractive in their turn.

But these new numbers were exceptionally constituted. The assisted immigrants of the two decades before the gold discoveries had included some people of skill, but they were on the whole, outside such special schemes as those of the South Australian Company, the products of the workhouses of Britain and Ireland. But statistics kept from 1854 show that from that year to the end of the decade, 23 per cent of new arrivals stating their occupations were skilled tradesmen and professional people, a much higher percentage than the 15 per cent of those going to the United States in the same years, and almost twice the 12½ per cent of skilled and professional people among the immigrants to Australia and New Zealand from 1860 to 1870. Such an immigration did more than increase population; it transformed its composition, and its outlooks, and in Victoria most of all.

At the outset of the decade, these long-run effects were less obvious than the immediate dangers.

With California in mind, many people might well fear the consequences of the public announcement of gold discoveries in New South Wales and Victoria in 1851. The *Sydney Morning Herald* forecast 'calamities far more terrible than earthquakes or pestilence', and Lieutenant-Governor La Trobe of Victoria feared that that colony might 'parallel California in crime and disorder'.

It was fortunate that the first and less valuable discoveries were made in New South Wales. The older colony of close on 200,000 people was able to absorb its few thousand diggers without shock, and to establish at the beginning the precedent of official law and order on the gold-fields. Victoria faced a far more desperate problem, for it was smaller and its gold-fields were much richer. Between 1851 and 1861 its population soared from 77,000 to 540,000 while that of New South Wales rose less dramatically to 350,000.

The small band of officials and police, adequate perhaps for a quiet pastoral community, could not cope with such an invasion; and La Trobe's officials and police were as much subject to the gold-fever as other people. Inevitably, there was an increase of private crime and violence, and the influx of ex-convicts from Tasmania caused much alarm. But the precedent of public order on the diggings had been established in the smaller rushes of New South Wales. By frantic improvisation, public control was extended to those of Victoria and there was no general breakdown of law and order.

If the sudden immigration created problems, it also made possible their solution; for not all came to dig, and many who did, turned away to other employment as extravagant hopes were sobered by realities. By 1853 La Trobe was able to recruit a sufficient force to restore normal security in the town and on the gold-fields, though bushrangers remained troublesome in remoter parts. Most visitors were struck by the orderliness of behaviour on the diggings, in contrast with the reckless disorder they expected to find.

Yet all was in ferment. Canvas, bark and rough-hewn slabs solved the problem of accommodating new numbers in Melbourne and on the diggings, imperfectly, it is true, and at the cost of outbreaks of typhoid fever. Feeding the diggers gave new opportunity to farmers of South Australia and Tasmania, and to the squatters. To the latter the gold-rushes had seemed at first to spell ruin by depriving them of their labourers; but if they could not shear their flocks, they could sell them as meat, and once more flocks were overlanded, not now to new pastures, but to the crude slaughter-houses of canvas and bark townships in Victorian gullies.

Indeed, it was more profitable to supply the digger than to dig. The profits of cartage, at anything up to £120 per ton from Melbourne to Bendigo when rain turned unmade roads into quagmires, lifted many into the ranks of farmers, manufacturers and contractors for the public and private building of the new-swollen community. Storekeepers and publicans of the gold-fields waxed fatter than all but a handful of their clients. Merchants and shipping firms profited from a vastly increased trade, though they had their passing difficulties in the scarcity and high price of labour, in the desertion of sailors to the diggings, and in their own recklessness in glutting the market. Landlords and owners of properties in the town profited greatly when rents for the flimsiest cottage soared and land values in Melbourne rose above those of London and New York.

How far labourers and diggers as a whole shared in the new prosperity, it is difficult to say. For a few years, the wages of all types of labourers rose to levels that seemed fantastic to contemporaries; but soaring prices must have allowed little improvement in real wages. In the later years of the decade, wages fell as immigrants and ex-diggers swelled the labour supply.

As to the diggers, a minority did well and a very small number made fortunes in the earlier years. For many of both types, new-found wealth vanished as rapidly as it came, in the grog-shanties of the gold-fields or, more flamboyantly, in the champagne and 'drinks all round', the carriages and golden display, that gave the town of Melbourne its brief fever of theatrical gaiety. But some of the successful diggers, no doubt, added to that growing number of men of moderate means who created the impression of widely shared prosperity.

From the beginning, however, travellers to the diggings met diggers returning from them dispirited and disillusioned; and by 1854 the yield per man was falling sharply, though the number of diggers continued to increase until 1858. The report of a Victorian Goldfields Commission of 1854 declared that three-quarters of the diggers made only 'a narrow and precarious livelihood'.

Every digger was required to pay thirty shillings a month for a licence to dig. On the Ballarat field, with its deeper shafts of 100 to 150 feet, the costs of digging and the risks of failure were greater than elsewhere, the time of waiting for certainty of success or failure was longer, and tempers were more sensitive to irrelevant irritations. Licence hunts carried out by police, whose arrogance sometimes equalled their inexperience, created a dangerous division, the diggers as a community opposing the police and official authority.

Frustration of hopes and irritation of temper gave a temporary following to a minority of political radicals, English, Irish and European; and, in a rising tension between diggers and police, the diggers formed the Ballarat Reform League which added the familiar chartist programme to a demand to end the licence fees. A tactless hunt for unlicensed diggers coming on top of a series of minor brushes turned irritation into revolt. The diggers burned their licences and threw up an armed stockade flying the blue flag of 'the Republic of Victoria', spangled with the stars of the Southern Cross. On Sunday morning, 3 December 1854, troops stormed the stockade and, with the loss of some thirty lives, the Eureka Rebellion was ended.

The pot of exasperation had boiled over, and this brought legislative council and executive on the one hand, diggers on the other, to a more sober realism. An official inquiry into grievances had already been planned and was commissioned immediately. As a result of its report, the licence fee was replaced by an export duty on gold as a source of revenue, and by a miner's right which cost one pound a year and gave its holder the vote.

In fact, only one-eighth of the miners troubled to vote at the ensuing election of 1856, a fact which suggests that political demands were for most of them no more than a graft on the main stem of their grievances as diggers. Indeed, radicals had generally complained of the political apathy of the diggers, too absorbed in the pursuit of wealth to give thought to the struggle for political rights. The diggers were satisfied by the ending of the licence hunts and by the setting up of local courts elected by themselves to make rules for the administration of the fields and to adjudicate disputes.

The Eureka Stockade has often been regarded as a great symbolic event in Australian labour history. In fact, it was not a revolt of wage-earners against organized capital, but of small capitalists against official authority. Its history further illustrates the theme that colonial radicalism, when it was not merely a dying echo of the old world's battles, was more militant in tone than in substance. Consider this reply of Peter Lalor, leader of the diggers at Eureka, to some of his critics only two years later:

I would ask these gentlemen what they mean by the term 'democracy'? Do they mean chartism or communism or republicanism? If so, I never was, I am not now, nor do I ever intend to be a democrat. But if a democrat means opposition to a tyrranical press, a tyrannical people or a tyrannical government, then I have ever been, I am still, and ever will remain a democrat.

Yet the Eureka legend is not wholly misleading, and Lalor's reply gives a clue to its grain of truth. For the dominant note of his statement is the independence of the individual man. The report of the Gold-fields Commission stressed this quality of independence as the most general characteristic of the diggers, and it continued to be expressed for some time to come in their fight, through their mining courts, against the advance of large mining companies employing labour.

If the diggers as such ceased to take active part in political life after Eureka, the diggings were nevertheless a training ground in democratic attitudes. Here people of all types and stations rubbed shoulders in an equal pursuit of fortune, and this experience bred an assertion, or rather an assumption of equality, if not in possessions, at least in title to consideration and respect.

Moreover, the great increase of population bridged more completely the old gulfs between masters and servants. It did so not only because of the diversity of those parts of society from which the immigrants of this time came, and not only because of the sudden enrichment of the lucky minority. It bridged the gulf above all because of the variety of callings into which immigrants moved, whether they had come to dig, or, as in many cases, with no purpose of digging but attracted simply by the new reputation of the golden colonies. Particularly in Victoria, the swollen numbers required a great increase of services, and the new wealth could pay for them.

Government increased, police increased. Sheep stations were fenced to save labour and more land was brought into farming use. Roads and railways were built or begun. Schools had to be put up and teachers found for them; and the proud if young colonies went further to provide themselves, even in a time of building shortage and of high costs of labour and materials, with two universities and with public libraries and numerous 'mechanics' institutes'.

Newspapers increased in circulation and the number of people they employed. The Melbourne *Argus* in 1848 was a small paper appearing twice weekly with a circulation of 625, and its weekly expenses were about £30. In 1852 its daily circulation was over 10,000 copies and it employed 140 hands.

Beyond all this the colonies increased their equipment of houses, hotels and even hospitals, of wharves and warehouses and all the services of city and port, of sewers and gas and water supply. The great majority of diggers and other immigrants, no doubt, swelled the ranks of labourers; but transforming minorities diversified and strengthened the middle ranks from skilled artisan and clerk to professional man, merchant and contractor.

A striking feature of this development was its highly urban character. Export income was earned by the rural producers of wool and hides, and, later in the century, wheat supported by fluctuating earnings from mining; but investment went overwhelmingly into urban development and into transport and communications. Australians became increasingly and remarkably dwellers in cities and towns. Some of the cities were of considerable size, Sydney and Melbourne ranking in population in the latter half of the nineteenth century with such cities as Rome and Baltimore. By 1901 Melbourne and Sydney each contained close on half a million people, Melbourne housing 41 per cent of Victoria's population and Sydney 35 per cent of the inhabitants of New South Wales.

At the other end of the scale, inadequately bridged by the few large towns—sea-port or mining towns such as Newcastle, Geelong and Ballarat—were the many small towns of one or two thousand people.

Large or small, these were the centres, to their varying degrees, of the expenditure of money, largely borrowed overseas, which, with some interruption in the 1890s, supported the continuing growth of the eastern colonies from 1860 to the outbreak of war in 1914. This expenditure went into city and suburban building and services and into communications within and between them. Within one decade, 1851 to 1860, Victoria's annual expenditure on roads and bridges rose from £11,000 to £3,163,000.

The share of government expenditure in the development of these decades was, as this example suggests, of particular importance when transport and communications, urban services, education and health became to an increasing degree the subjects of state responsibility and therefore of state expenditure.

Increasing reliance on government did not prevent the diverse development of these decades from strengthening a quality in the colonial atmosphere on which newcomers remarked. This was a sense of freedom and flexibility. Even though their attachment to old Europe might be strong, they had often a feeling of being less earthbound by tradition, of being more easily able to alter established things, such as their inherited condition or traditional institutions. It is quite true that this feeling often lashed itself somewhat impotently into disillusionment against real bars of economic or political privilege. But the belief was continually renewed, and fed that faith in Australia Unlimited which was so strong a colonial trait in this and later times.

That sense of equality and freedom was discussed at length by William Westgarth, founder and first president of the Melbourne Chamber of Commerce, wise chairman of the Commission of Inquiry into the Eureka troubles, and author of several penetrating books on colonial Australia. The following extracts from his *Victoria: Late Australia Felix*, written at the height of the gold-rushes in 1853, will illustrate the theme.

Change of fortune is the constant feature of a thriving colony. The change is not always for the better, but it is so in the great proportion of cases—a circumstance that imparts alike vigour and exciting novelty to the social picture. Hope is ever conspicuous in the mind of the Victorian, imparting all its vivacious characteristics; and the Australian climate has often monopolized the whole credit for a joyousness of life that is due, in part at least, to the effect of other Australian circumstances. . . .

Colonial society is pre-eminently practical and utilitarian. This must be expected where no ancient local usages or institutions influence another course. It is the course of common sense, and one altogether unavoidable among the intelligent masses in a new sphere. Our colonies are certainly republics whenever they separate from the parent state. To conceive them pondering over any other form of government, and deliberately instituting those inequalities of old societies that have acquired their root in remote time and in a totally different condition of society, is an idea entirely foreign to our age and people. These inequalities of long-established governments bear up successfully against the levelling pressure of modern progress by virtue of circumstances which have never existed in colonies, and which cannot be created now by commands either from within or from without . . . nor is it reasonable to suppose that the laborious fabric of a thousand years' adjustment can be transferred like so much railway machinery to run without 'accidents' upon the new Australian as upon the old British line. The effort to engraft such inequalities tends merely to agitate and divide society. . . .

The social equalities of colonies give them an aspect of rudeness to eyes that are fresh from the mother country. But this first impression, although in some respects a true one, affords only a superficial view of the whole case. This rudeness of aspect is the necessary result of a general prosperity that brings all classes to some similar degree of independence and consideration. . . . The independent bearing of the colonial labouring population, in short of the whole of the employed classes, is often commented upon. A labourer in Australia is indeed a very different personage from one in the mother country, and he is not long of knowing the fact.

Later experience did not make Westgarth change his mind. So, ten years later, he explained the rapid granting of manhood suffrage in Victoria as simply a recognition of facts; '. . . the existence of the manhood suffrage measure is not the cause of Victoria's democracy; it is only one of the normal results; it is the adjusting of the political to the social constitution'.

So, in part, it was; and those in possession of political privileges gave way a little and shared them, within limits and with frequent misgiving. Some justified their action on the ground that the wide distribution of at least a fair livelihood would prevent the deep social hatreds of the old world from growing in the new. The more sceptical could remember that there were checks on hasty democracy still, by way of unequal electorates and propertied upper houses. Nevertheless, by the end of the 'fifties, the colonists at large, except in Western Australia, had gained the power to assert their legislative wishes with some chance of eventual success, although they were to learn with some bitterness in the land selection struggle, that the battle might merely have been transferred to other fields.

They used their power without delay and with vigour, proceeding to reshape the colonies in their own image, the image of the small and would-be independent man. They did not set out to reshape society according to preconceived and comprehensive theory, but did so incidentally in the course of solving particular and immediate problems and grievances. These can all be reduced to the problem of providing secure employment for swollen numbers, together with some degree of independence if possible, and at any rate at a fair level of livelihood.

8

AGGRESSIVE DEMOCRACY, 1860–1900

During the second half of the nineteenth century, the accepted creed of Australian society came to be the belief 'that every man should start fair in life, and have the same chance of making his way through the world'. That statement was made, not by a professed radical, but by a Victorian conservative; for there were few in the colonies, even among those who were termed conservatives—and fewer as the century neared its close—who would openly defend inherited inequalities.

In the earlier part of the period of this chapter, that belief was most vigorously asserted in the three colonies of New South Wales, Victoria and South Australia, because it was those colonies that had received large numbers of free immigrants in the 'fifties who sought, not merely jobs, but jobs which might justify their migration.

Whether the cry was to unlock the pastoral lands for yeoman farmers, or to nourish colonial industries behind tariff walls that were expected to protect both industry and the artisan alike; or whether it was to keep out the Chinese and all cheap labour, or to provide education for all; these various demands combined in a picture of an Australia which should, first and foremost, offer a high standard of livelihood and opportunity to its people at large.

It was an ideal which did not so much eliminate the uncommon man as neglect him. Yet, as it was felt by its proponents, it was not always a mediocre and limited ideal. The vast optimism of Australia Unlimited transformed it, and the belief was widespread that if these minimum guarantees were secured, greater things might follow. Australia was 'free from the clogs and accumulated hindrances which act as drags upon the progress of other countries; . . . we, having nothing to undo can, if we will, make the last page of their history the first of our own, and complete to its finished perfection the temple of which they have but laid the solid foundations'.

It was to take long and disillusioning experience before we learned that our continent could not provide a comfortable existence for unlimited millions of people and that the crossing of the oceans could not release us from the bonds of history. But at this time, immigration had weakened old acquiescence, and the sudden expansion of the colonies in the gold decade and their rapid winning of a large measure of democracy bred confidence in their power to mould things to their liking.

The flame of democratic idealism did not burn with undimmed brightness throughout this period, and colonial politics in the 'seventies and 'eighties often degenerated into a petty manœuvring for place and profit. In any case, even idealists were to learn that their dearest schemes could be foiled by upper houses defending the interests of property, and that even when this obstacle was overcome there was a large gap between the aims and the achievements of legislation.

In the gold decade itself, the urgent task was to find alternative and secure livelihood for a suddenly swollen population as the diggings declined. Agitation to this end was sustained by acute unemployment in Victoria and New South Wales from 1857 to 1866 and followed the twin paths of wresting land for small farmers from the squatters and protecting native industries. In fact any achievement—and it was limited—came far too late to solve the immediate problem of finding work for ex-diggers. They found it in migration to other colonies and in the predominantly urban development already referred to. Victoria's first tentative nibble at protection in 1866, followed by a full measure of it in 1879, did not deflect the path of development, while settlement on the land, which had to await railways to be effective, never involved any large proportion of the population. Building, road and railway construction and services absorbed the men who grew old while the agitation, which began with plans for providing them with smiling farms and protected industries, continued. Long before the gold-rushes, radical writers had, in imagination, peopled the pastoral emptiness with small and always smiling homesteads. The demand to unlock the pastoral lands and 'to rear a staunch and honest race of independent yeomen' now became the most popular solution to the problem of numbers. A block of land seemed to offer the combination of livelihood and independence that the diggers so greatly valued. But if the demand had this beckoning vision behind it, it was sustained, as often, by a more negative fear of privilege. Of this the squatters were seen as the chief incumbents defended by the twin walls of their actual occupation of the land and of their power in the upper houses.

South Australia was able to meet the demand for land without serious social rifts. Indeed, in this period, South Australia seemed to demonstrate the ideal character, the form, of nineteenth-century democracy in Australia.

Its farming and mining communities vied on equal terms of experience and importance with its pastoralists who at no time gained the predominance in that colony which they had gained in New South Wales and to a more limited extent in Victoria. Moreover, South Australia contained an exceptionally high proportion of nonconformists—almost 60 per cent compared with 30 per cent in New South Wales—whose traditional independence of spirit was re-enforced by the considerable number of South Australians who returned there from the Victorian gold-fields.

For all these reasons, South Australia displayed a flexible, experimental democracy less marked by a sense of class hostility than in New South Wales and Victoria. So it was able to meet the demand for land with laws that were readily modified in the light of experience and changing circumstance.

In New South Wales and Victoria the problem was more difficult. In these two colonies, democracy was not more progressive than in South Australia, but in the early years of the period it was inevitably more militant. For here the protagonists of democratic programmes were faced with the much more powerful opposition of the pastoralists. The necessity of knocking down squatters in order to raise farmers added to their determination, but weakened their flexibility, their readiness to work out the practicable compromises that came more easily in South Australia.

It was clear that land for farmers would in the first instance have to be taken from the squatters; for the unoccupied lands were in large part unsuitable by reason of their aridity or remoteness, or presented, in such regions as the mallee with its tough wiry scrub and Gippsland with its giant forests, even greater difficulties to farmers of the first generation than to pastoralists. Inevitably, attempts to resume occupied lands from the squatters were resisted as acts of confiscation. They might hold their lands by lease or licence of limited duration; but they were theirs by natural justice, they felt, if not by law.

Strongly entrenched still in the colonial upper houses, the squatters were able during the 'fifties to reject several land bills; and, set against the background of the simultaneous struggle for political rights, their opposition turned the development of agriculture into a social question when it was to prove still more a matter of mastering difficulties of soil, climate and distance. Embittered social hostility was unfavourable to attempts in these earlier years to find some reasonable demarcation between areas suitable for agriculture and those in which pasture might well be left undisturbed.

The weight of the demand was too great to be long resisted, and between 1861 and 1869 the parliaments of New South Wales and Victoria passed a number of selection acts designed to encourage intending farmers to select blocks of land in the pastoral areas which they might gain in fee simple by paying a purchase price in instalments and by fulfilling certain conditions of occupancy and improvement.

Legislative victory after struggle bred an easy optimism: 'Now the Land Bill has passed and the good time has come.' The results brought disillusion in large measure. Neither the number of farmers nor the area of cultivation was increased in proportion to the number of selectors and the amount of land alienated under the selection acts.

In New South Wales between 1861 and 1883 over 15,000,000 acres were alienated and the area of cultivated land was increased by only 300,000 acres. Some part of the remainder had passed into the hands of selectors who eked out the miserable rewards of grazing a few sheep and cows by finding seasonal work as shearers and bush workers. But a very large part had passed into the possession of its squatter occupants who had been able to manipulate the land laws in their own favour.

The Victorian Acts were more successful, and the area of cultivation increased by over 1,000,000 acres between 1861 and 1880. Nevertheless, before revised Acts of 1865 and 1869 imposed stricter conditions, large parts of the rich western district had passed as freehold into the hands of the squatters under the terms of earlier selection laws.

Neither squatter nor selector had a monopoly of the extensive misuse of these laws. If the squatter could hire 'dummies' to select key spots of his run on his behalf, he was also at the mercy of blackmailing pseudo-selectors, who intended, not to farm their selections, but to force the squatter to buy them off at a stiff price.

Such malpractices apart, the cards were stacked against the genuine selector. The selection acts were primarily intended to put the small man on the land. But farming, whatever the terms on which land might be granted, required capital for clearing, fencing and stocking the farm and to pay for equipment and labour. A large proportion of the selectors had little or no capital, and were forced, since they were too poor security for the banks, to borrow at high rates from storekeepers, stock-and-station agents and some less reputable money-lenders. Many were forced by indebtedness to surrender their holdings to newcomers and carried their bitterness into the ranks of the shearers and drovers, the fencers and rouse-abouts of the outback.

Others were tempted by the land acts into areas which were unsuitable for agriculture through lack of water or transport. For one reason and another, miserable slow defeat stood often in stark contrast with the optimism which greeted the land acts.

The squatters did not escape unscathed. They could borrow more readily and were able to gain the freehold of large parts of their runs on terms intended to aid agriculture. But they did so at a cost of debt, which reduced their power to resist the onset of drought and falling prices towards the end of the century, and which caused them to overstock, with damage to their pastures. Moreover, the struggle cost them their old prestige, and for a long time they played a smaller part in the political leadership of Australia than their role in the country's economy would warrant.

The struggle also lowered respect for law in wide sections of the community. A royal commission reported:

> It has tarnished the personal virtues of veracity and honourable dealing by the daily habit of intrigue, by the practice of evading the law, and by declarations in defiance of fact universally made. Self-interest has created a laxity of conscience in all matters connected with the land laws, and the stain attaches to men of all classes and all degrees.

Professor Shann's thesis in his *Economic History of Australia* is probably correct, that the social feuds between squatters and selectors and the habit of perjury encouraged the revival of bushranging in the 'seventies and 'eighties. The most disturbing aspect of this outbreak of violence was the fact that large numbers of people looked on indifferent or hostile as the police attempted to check it; '. . . free selection before survey', writes Shann, 'made the tasks of the police and the schoolmasters uphill and dangerous work'. For if it was the policeman's task to capture the bushranger, it was the school-master's task to teach the feud-ridden rural population the principles of law and order.

Time, however, was on the side of both policeman and school-master. The generation of social conflict over 'free selection' gave way to one of more successful 'closer settlement' which blurred old bitterness and bred a more settled rural population. In the 'nineties it was observed that farmers, who had previously been a radical group, mainly in opposition to the conservative influence of the squatters, were moving into a common front with them against urban parties which showed a taste for land taxes.

The conflicts over the land laws have often obscured the fact that this same period wrought a revolution in Australian farming. Its essence was the discovery that fallow, repeatedly worked to give a good tilth, conserved nitrates and moisture for the next crop. This method of 'dry farming' enabled a migration of wheat-growing from the cooler, wetter coastal areas, earlier favoured, to the drier inland areas of the present wheat-belt.

In the devising of methods of farming dry country, the colony of South Australia led the way. Its wheat areas were a bridge between the approximately English conditions of Tasmania, which had been the colonial granary until 1850, and the quite un-English districts of the later wheat-belt. The soils of even those districts earliest used for wheat in South Australia were similar to those later used for wheat in Victoria and New South Wales, and their limited summer drought gave a comparatively gentle training in the vicissitudes of wheat-growing in dry country.

Since the inland districts gave lighter yields, the farmer had to work a larger area for every bushel of grain he harvested; and his costs were by that measure increased. This was a spur to the invention and use of mechanical devices to save labour and cheapen costs. Ridley's stripper, invented in South Australia in 1843, was coming into general use in the 'sixties, and was improved into a complete harvester which stripped, winnowed and bagged the grain in one process. Other inventions such as the 'stump-jump plough' and the 'mullenizer' or log roller enabled farmers to clear the tough scrub of the mallee country with less back-breaking labour and to cultivate it while it was still only partly cleared.

One of the main obstacles to the Australian farmer's participation in the world wheat trade was the cost of transporting his grain to the ports. The inland shift of the wheat-belt depended on the building of railways to provide cheap freights. Though governments entered the business reluctantly, and not in any fervour of state socialism, the building and running of railways early became a function of government. Vast distances and a thin-strewn population were unfavourable to private enterprise, and governments were first drawn into railway building to rescue private companies from their difficulties.

Victoria, with greater capital and population, was building actively in the 'fifties and 'sixties, and its railways had reached the Murray by 1879 and the South Australian border by 1885. It was along these lines that Victorian farming successfully competed with grazing in the years of the selection struggles. The great railway age in Australia was, however, the two decades from 1870 to 1890. In 1870 there were 1,000 miles of railway in Australia; in 1890 there were 10,800 miles, the building of which had been in large part financed by government loans raised in London.

In the concluding years of this period there was much wasteful and unremunerative building, and colonial separatism had burdened the country with costly and irritating changes of gauge. However, this building of railways made possible the quickened expansion of wheat farming which followed. Meanwhile it had been established as an axiom of government policy that railways should be a public service rather than a profitable investment, and low freights for rural produce became a form of state subsidy to the farming and pastoral communities.

The great development of wheat farming after 1890 depended on two further conditions. During the last thirty years of the century, yields in the longer-worked South Australian wheat districts were declining disastrously. Professor Custance of Roseworthy College, an agricultural college established by the South Australian Government in 1879, had pointed to a cause, the shortage of phosphates in Australian soils, and had advised farmers to dress the land with soluble superphosphates. Farmers were slow to listen, but when they did so, dressing with 'super' saved them.

The other condition was the breeding of wheats adapted to Australian conditions. Before 1890 farmers had used English and some South African strains. No doubt varieties descended from these wheats had adapted themselves to Australian conditions to some degree by a process of natural selection. In 1886, William Farrer, a Cambridge mathematician, began experiments near the present capital of Australia in breeding quick-ripening and drought-resisting wheats which would give better average returns in the variable conditions of the Australian wheat-belt. He was the pioneer of work which has not ceased.

Meanwhile, Australian agriculture was being diversified by more intensive types of cultivation. Wine-growing was almost as old as settlement, but in the last twenty years of the century the invention of refrigeration machinery made it possible to export Australian butter, fruit and meat to the other side of the world. In this same period, various irrigation schemes were undertaken by private individuals and local water trusts, particularly on the Murray and its Victorian tributaries. As so often in our history, it was found that only central governments had the resources to develop large schemes effectively, and in the twentieth century, irrigation became a function of the State.

In retrospect it is clear that agricultural advance depended as much on the conquest of natural difficulties as on victory over the squatters; but it had appeared in the earlier years mainly as a conflict for possession of the land. In the same period, that conflict was paralleled, most of all in Victoria, by a conflict between free-traders and protectionists which also took on the appearance of uncompromising social struggle.

In both struggles the appearance of class-war may be exaggerated. Those who led the fight for land and for protection, though they appealed to the propertyless populace, were themselves merchants and newspaper proprietors, industrialists, miners and professional men, who in the one case were simply attacking a monopoly and in the other case seeking certain conditions of industrial development. Militancy of temper there was in plenty; but their demands were particular and limited.

The demand for protective tariffs succeeded in Victoria probably because its gold-rush immigration and forced pace of growth had stimulated an unusual variety of industries ready to seek protection as demand slackened. But the cause already voiced in the 'fifties also found its man in David Syme, proprietor of the Melbourne newspaper, *The Age*. Syme took up protection as his main cause, appealing beyond the industrialist to the labouring classes by constantly reiterating the view that a tariff wall would protect not only industry but the industrial worker. It was in the prolonged and heated discussions about protection that the idea of a 'fair and reasonable' standard of living for all became the axiom to which respect must be paid in all Australian political controversy and social legislation.

In the course of the controversy, arguments of political economy were swamped by arguments of a purely political kind; for, as squatter and importer opponents of protection commanded a majority in the Upper House, the question of protection was merged into the continuing struggle for reform of the Upper House. The first halting protective tariff of 1866 was enacted only after a bitter deadlock between the houses had induced both sides to retreat a little into compromise. Not until 1879 had Victoria committed itself beyond recall to protection.

While Victoria became aggressively protectionist, New South Wales remained righteously free-trade. For New South Wales had smaller numbers to settle in employment, larger areas of undeveloped country, a revenue kept buoyant by land sales, and a sound basis in its coal-fields for industrial development. Nevertheless, protectionists were a powerful minority even in New South Wales.

In the 'seventies and early 'eighties there was on the whole a dimming of the reforming zeal of the earlier years. Great battles for political rights, for land, and, in Victoria, for protection, had been won. In large measure, victory had disillusioned the victors; for experience had made it evident that legislation alone was not enough to create the promised land. Charles Gavan Duffy, weary of political battle and looking backwards to Europe and the youthful idealism of his Irish days, was not alone when he wrote at this time, 'We shall not create a new Arcadia in these pastoral lands, labour we ever so zealously.'

In part the decline of reforming enthusiasm was a measure of the expanding prosperity of these years. It was a measure, also, of the spreading acceptance of common assumptions, the absence of major conflicts of principle. The colonists used the familiar labels, 'conservative' and 'liberal', though parties were slow to develop; but these terms, as many realized, were misleading. There were few conservatives who defended the concept of a traditional, hierarchical society; and the difference was hardly more than this, that 'liberals' would go a little farther and a little faster.

Party labels were in any case misleading because parties given cohesion by a proclaimed platform and an accepted discipline, did not exist until the closing years of the century. The prolonged campaign for protection did give Victoria some earlier anticipations of party discipline in which the fidelity of parliamentary members to the proclaimed programme of reform was to some degree ensured by extra-parliamentary associations in the constituencies. But even in Victoria parties remained embryonic into the 'eighties, and in all the eastern colonies, parliament in the first generation of responsible government was managed, not by parties, but by factions. Members naturally grouped themselves about a number of leaders, no one of whom could hope to gain a majority except by coalition with other leaders and their followers. Bargaining and the use of various forms of influence enabled certain practised leaders to build up majorities, and even to hold them. So long as prosperity and continuing material development masked the discords of society, this system could work with reasonable efficiency.

During the 1880s, however, prosperity was ceasing to be eternally predictable, even if speculation on the Melbourne stock market soared to still dizzier heights. Expansion was set in a context of falling world prices, which brought an early and salutary taste of depression to South Australia.

In these more difficult times, the old pattern of politics by bargaining ceased to be acceptable. At the least, the old faction leaders, in the words of Loveday and Martin (*Parliament, Factions and Parties*) 'reluctantly came to terms with emerging political movements which they could use, but not control'. They might even find their spheres of influence invaded by new parties in which they had no place at all. Sir Henry Parkes's position in 1889 as leader of the new Liberal Party of New South Wales is one example of the change; for he was leader, on the party's terms, of an organised party which anticipated the discipline of Labour with its constituency associations, its central executive and its platform pledge. The new Labour Parties, before the realities of parliamentary experience taught Labour leaders themselves the arts of the faction leader, were a more complete sign of the change from faction to party.

Even in the pre-party days of piecemeal bargaining, democratic militancy readily stirred when upper houses proved obstinate in the defence of privilege; and in one field, that of public education, a genuine democratic idealism won victories even in these years of declining enthusiasm. Utilitarian though the dominant note of colonial society inevitably was, there had always been those who were stirred by the lack of the cultural amenities of the old world to give time and labour to their creation in the new.

By such efforts, Hobart in the 'thirties and 'forties had been made a centre of intellectual light in the colonial darkness until prolonged economic stagnation and the penal system quenched it. The 'fifties were years of great cultural enthusiasm. In 1850, New South Wales established the first Australian university with liberal provision to enable the talented son of poor parents to enter it. If Wentworth, its main founder, believed in aristocracy, he also believed in the right of worth and talent to graduate into it.

In the midst of the turmoil of the gold-rushes, Victoria rapidly created a university, a public library, an art gallery and a museum, while the intellectual thirst of colonists in several colonies was seen in the creation of mutual improvement societies, philosophical societies and institutions for the advancement of science. In many an Australian country town today, a languishing Mechanics' Institute survives in diminished evidence of the cultural fervour of that time. Today, there are once again signs of a revival of local cultural activity, the product of many years of missionary work in adult education and of a great development of army education during the last war.

With a faith in the beneficent influence of popular education which sometimes drew strength from their own hard struggles to get it, men like Henry Parkes worked in all the colonies during the period of this chapter to bring primary and secondary education within reach of children of all classes and of all areas.

Education [declared Parkes in a passage that makes clear the nature of his radicalism] will make people acquainted with their rights and mindful of their duties. . . . It is equally hostile to anarchy and despotism. . . . It alone has the power to awaken the humbler classes to a true sense of the dignity of humanity, and inspire them with a true love of equality and order combined, which is the true foundation of freedom.

The sudden growth of population in the 'fifties had made the provision of schools and teachers on a larger scale an urgent need. Their Irish adherents apart, liberals and radicals hardened towards a belief in government-controlled secular schools. This was less a matter of liberal secularism than of circumstance. There was no one established church in the colonies, and sectarian bitterness was kept alive as new immigrants brought with them old-world divisions that were on the whole less religious than national, less a matter of Anglicans, Presbyterians, and Roman Catholics than of English, Scots, and Irish. An earlier 'dual system' of national and denominational schools, both subsidized by governments, had encouraged rivalry without satisfying the need.

The outcome after years of conflict was the principle of 'free, compulsory and secular' education, first adopted in Victoria in 1872—free, to make it available to all; compulsory, to force in particular its provision for the scattered population of the interior; and secular, in the hope of cutting a way through sectarian differences. In time, all the colonies discontinued subsidies to church schools, set up public departments of education and made schooling free or almost so. The churches, and especially the Roman Catholic Church, continued to run their own schools, but without subsidy.

It was a mark of the weakness of local government that public education was from the first controlled by departments of the central governments. If this has made for an excess of standardization, bureaucratic control and public indifference, at the time it was the only method of ensuring an adequate provision of schools for all areas, and of securing reasonably high and even standards of training for teachers. In these aims, it succeeded.

The 'seventies and 'eighties were a time of great material development. London financial houses subscribed readily to colonial government loans for large projects of developmental works. Private capital flowed in as readily to colonial banks and land, building, and finance companies.

Well into the 'eighties this inflow of overseas capital nourished remunerative enterprise; but easy money bred carelessness in both government and private enterprises. Between 1886 and 1890, the colonies were importing capital at a rate of £20,000,000 a year, and in those years, a larger proportion of government expenditure went into unnecessary and unremunerative works while private capital fed a frenzy of speculation and display.

Floods in Queensland, droughts in New South Wales and South Australia, together with some premonitory failures, checked speculation earlier in those colonies. But Victoria was the financial capital of the continent and a centre for reinvestment in the other colonies. In this colony the speculative boom continued longer and reached dizzier heights; and the fall was greater.

This speculation underlined the predominantly urban and suburban character of investment in the eastern colonies. It was in these years that Melbourne's citizens built for all time at a cost of £20,000 to £30,000 apiece the Italianate mansions which this generation has been pulling down to make way for multiple flats and less spacious living. The genuine prosperity of the time was inflated into a fevered boom by land and finance companies which sprouted like mushrooms in the 'eighties and made money available on long and easy terms to those who wished to buy or build.

Building, buying, lavish entertainment and speculation rested on the assumption that the great prosperity of the time was normal and would continue. But that prosperity was under-pinned by three insecure props—high export incomes, the continuance of public loans and works on a large scale, and the continuing ability of the colonists to pay inflated prices for the lands and houses and services they were being offered. At the beginning of the 'nineties, all three props collapsed.

Prices of all colonial exports fell sharply between 1884 and 1893, and wool prices continued low until 1897, with a resulting fall in incomes and employment. That result was cushioned somewhat by borrowing and public works. But the Argentinian failures of 1890 and the near failure of Baring's bred in London financial houses a suspicion of all colonial ventures which was heightened by the failure of Melbourne's largest building society so proudly named the Premier Permanent Building Society, and by the stories of reckless speculation which its failure made public.

Colonial governments, which, if not spotless in their control of expenditure, had shown no sign of repudiation, were hard put to it to borrow enough to meet impending repayments and their public works were suddenly and severely curtailed, with great loss of employment and income to people of all classes. The onset of general depression brought forty-one land and building companies tumbling down in 1891–2, and by the middle of 1893 thirteen of the twenty-five banks doing business in Australia had suspended payment and gone into reconstruction.

Into the uneasy atmosphere on the eve of this crash there burst the maritime strike of 1890 which ushered in four years of industrial disputes of a scale and bitterness without precedent in the colonies.

The bitterness of these strikes may obscure the fact that the unions and those members of parliament who spoke for them laid their stress on the co-operation of capital and labour. This was true of the new intercolonial unions which had spread so rapidly in the 'eighties as it was of the older and smaller craft unions. W. G. Spence, architect of the Amalgamated Miners' Association and the Australian Shearers' Union, told the Intercolonial Trade Union Congress of 1884, 'They all recognized the usefulness of capital, and all present, he was sure, desired to work amicably with the employers of labour. . . . Experience had shown that trades unions, instead of injuring employers, operated to their advantage'. That argument was typical.

It is true that the unions fought a large number of strikes before 1890. These, however, were not manœuvres in a war on capitalist society; they were strikes to establish the right of the unions to exist and to speak for the workmen, or to gain piecemeal improvements. It is true, also, that the task of forming intercolonial unions and of enrolling large numbers of workers who had previously not been organized required and stimulated missionary zeal, and at that time militancy was more easily heard, and may indeed have been of greater influence than the quieter affirmations of harmony.

Militancy was given a millennial flavour by the popularity of Edward Bellamy's Utopian fantasy, *Looking Backward* and by the writings of the English-born socialist, William Lane, who settled in Queensland in 1883, and in *The Boomerang* and *The Worker* wrote fervent calls for a socialist remoulding of Australia. He was widely read, particularly by the bush workers; but what he taught was enthusiasm and solidarity—'Socialism is just being mates'—rather than a revolutionary ideology. The greatest doctrinal influence on the workers was Henry George, whose 'single tax' gained a considerable following.

Despite this and despite the great strikes of 1890–4, traditional piecemeal bargaining was not transformed into a fight to reconstruct society at a stroke, though the revivalist feeling and the revivalist language of such a fight were common enough. Indeed, neither the initial enthusiasm of the strikers nor the establishment of the political Labour Party in 1891 after their defeat would be explicable without this reforming drive, and it owed as much to hope as to disillusionment. But the belief in co-operation continued after defeat and after the full-dress entry of labour into politics, and it could do so because a socialist fervour could exist separate from a complete and unyielding doctrine of class-war.

In 1889, however, co-operation was faltering. The intercolonial unions of workmen were matched by intercolonial associations of employers, and the employers on their side were feeling the pinch of falling prices and were ready to challenge the unions. The unions were stronger in zeal than in numbers, experience or tactics; for they did not comprise all workers and spreading depression was creating a large body of unemployed who could be used as strike breakers.

The great strikes of 1890–4 involved workers of many industries in Australia and New Zealand—seamen, wharf-labourers, carters, shearers and miners. Through all the variations of particular issues, the struggle was essentially between the employers' insistence on 'freedom of contract' which would have destroyed the 'new unionism', and the unions' demand for the 'closed shop', i.e. for collective bargaining by the unions on behalf of all workers. In all cases the unions were defeated and obliged to return to work on the employers' terms.

The strikes did not create the depression, which had other causes. Nor did defeat in the strikes first cause the unions to turn to politics, though it hastened the formation of a permanent Labour Party. There had been a number of labour members in the colonial parliaments in earlier years, some of them subsidized by Trades Hall Councils as delegates in the labour interest. But the militant and utopian socialist fervour generated in the formation of the new unions, such as the Amalgamated Miners' Association and Australian Shearers' Union quickened the demand, at least in New South Wales and Queensland, for a party directly representing labour. And both the militancy and organisation of the unions gave the new 'Labour Parties' in those two colonies a unity and strength not normally found in the faction politics which had hitherto been normal. It is true that this unity had to be rediscovered when Labour members split on traditional issues. It is further true, as Dr Robin Gollan has demonstrated in his *Radical and Working Class Politics*, that if 'from militant trade unionism and socialist theory the Labour Party acquired a unity, . . . it used the strength springing from that unity to put into effect policies that were neither militant nor socialist' —the policies, in fact, of traditional radicals and liberals. From this arose a continuing struggle between the political labour party, drawn towards relatively cautious amendment, and the more militant sections of the industrial movement, impatient of politicians' electoral calculations.

The rapid rise of political labour in the 'nineties owed much to the troubles of those years. It also owed much to the failure of the established politicians to rise to the level of their responsibilities. For in the years of crisis, these politicians were in large measure tried and found wanting by many who were not themselves unionists but who shared the common assumption that 'every man should start fair in life'.

It is true that Sir George Dibbs's government in New South Wales took prompt and decisive measures to restore the credit of the banks, in contrast with the Victorian premier, J. B. Patterson's, despairing cry, 'We are all floundering'. It is true, too, that in some of the colonies, the first steps were taken by the established parties as well as by Labour, towards industrial conciliation and arbitration, emploers' liability for accidents to workmen, and the control of sweated industries. In the 1890s, New South Wales, Queensland, Victoria and South Australia all passed factory legislation, much of which introduced elements of compulsion in the control of working hours and conditions.

But unemployment was regarded as either a temporary accident or deserved, and governments did not go beyond grudging subsidy to charitable organizations and some ill-conceived relief works to serious consideration of unemployment as a problem requiring official policy. Towards the close of the century, New South Wales and Victoria, under pressure from the Labour Party, introduced old-age pensions; but, in general, social relief was still widely regarded as likely to undermine the independence of the workman and in such matters the attachment of the traditional parties to *laissez faire* went deeper.

Their greatest failure in the crisis years was their failure to spread sacrifice evenly between middle and labouring classes in the measures taken to balance tottering budgets. Mild taxes on land and income, passed with difficulty, imposed on established wealth no burden that was proportionate to the burden imposed on people of low incomes by retrenchments of the salaries of public servants and teachers, even down to those on £100 a year, and in Victoria by increased duties on common necessities such as tea.

Despite droughts from 1894 to the terrible desolation of 1902, recovery had begun before the end of the century. Depression ended speculation and forced a return to pioneering. New South Wales and Queensland with great undeveloped resources were quickly expanding again; in South Australia, speculation had been checked and worse disasters prevented by droughts in the early 'eighties, while Tasmania and Western Australia had been little touched by the depression and were entering a long-delayed period of expansion. For mining continued to develop strongly through the worst years, and the discovery of silver-lead and copper in Tasmania and of gold in Western Australia brought moderate prosperity to the former and a dramatic transformation to the latter. The value of Western Australia's production of gold rose from £86,663 in 1890 to £6,000,000 in 1900, and its population was increased during the same period, mainly by immigration from the eastern colonies, from 46,000 to 179,000.

Looked at as a whole, the half-century since 1850 had been one of great material growth. The 400,000 people who lived in the colonies in 1851 had jumped to over 1,000,000 in 1861 and were approaching 4,000,000 in 1901. They had equipped themselves with 13,000 miles of railways and extended the area of cultivated land from under 500,000 acres to close on 10,000,000 acres, with another 15,000,000 of planted pastures. The 17,000,000 sheep of 1851 had increased to a peak of 106,000,000 in 1891, to be reduced by the droughts, however, almost to half that number in 1902.

Meanwhile, the colonies had varied their economy with a wide range of industrial undertakings, though for the most part these were small in scale still, and most concentrated in the two colonies, Victoria and New South Wales. But the 2,000 industrial employees or thereabouts of 1850 had multiplied to well over 400,000 at the end of the century, and went near to equalling those employed in primary production. Despite the setbacks of the closing decade which were made good fairly rapidly, the value of external trade had risen from about £5,000,000 in 1850 to £90,000,000 in 1901.

Most marked in the expansion of this time was the growth of large cities. By the close of the century, the capital cities housed one-third of the population of the colonies, and the proportion of city dwellers was increasing. Sydney and Melbourne had grown from small colonial townships into cities of half a million inhabitants each. Australians continued to think of themselves as pioneers of a rural wilderness when in fact they were to a large and increasing extent city born and city bred—though they have been rarely city lovers.

The high proportion of town dwellers is to be explained by geography which has allowed only a sparse occupation of the interior, and concentrated both population and communications on the coastal rim. As industries developed, they followed the prevailing fashion, to be near local markets and established transport, and to be near the main sources of power. It has been for almost a century as usual as it is idle to deplore this concentration of people in sea-board towns. The process may be somewhat modified by official aid to decentralization and by the provision of electric power in rural districts; but it is not likely to be reversed.

Its most serious effect has been the slow and still anaemic growth of local government in Australia. This has limited the opportunity for people at large to share, beyond the ballot box, in the responsibilities of government, and it has thrown on central governments many services which in England are a function of local government.

At the close of the century, the six colonies joined in a federal union as the Commonwealth of Australia. Federation was the work of minorities which felt strongly about it and worked hard for it. But Australia was not swept into it on a wave of national enthusiasm, and it is probable that it succeeded as much by the relative absence, outside New South Wales, of determined and organised opposition. Those such as Deakin who worked for it might be deeply and solemnly convinced of its importance. Tom Roberts, the painter, described the opening of the first federal parliament as 'very solemn and great', and many felt this emotion at the moment. But the majority of Australians seem to have taken but a lukewarm interest in the movement, neither opposing nor promoting it strongly. Nevertheless their common characteristics and their common interests were stronger than their differences and jealousies.

The rivalry between free trade New South Wales and protectionist Victoria, and the fear of people in New South Wales that the tune might be called by the smaller states, were the greatest obstacles to federation. But against these dividing forces stood exasperation at border restrictions and the facts of co-operation in many spheres— in the conferences of colonial governments, in the intercolonial meetings of the trade unions, in intercolonial organizations of employers. In any case, Australians moved easily from colony to colony with little sense of strangeness.

Certain incidents brought home the weakness of division. Australian national sentiment was abruptly disturbed into vigour by the British Government's refusal to sanction Queensland's annexation of eastern New Guinea in 1883, and Australian fears were aroused by the German annexation of the northern half of that area in 1884. War scares in the 'eighties, and a British military expert's report of 1889 on the defence of the colonies gave further stimulus to the federation movement. The troubles of the 'nineties had afflicted most of the colonies alike and impressed many people with the need of common action to set the economic life of the country on a more stable basis.

Above all, there was no barrier of racial or national difference to keep the colonies apart. They had become fundamentally alike in their social and political structure and in their attachment to the assumptions of a democratic, egalitarian society.

There had been exceptions to this attachment up to the closing decade of the century. Only in the 'eighties and 'nineties did the discovery of minerals bring transforming numbers of free and independent-minded immigrants from the other colonies to Tasmania and Western Australia. Before that time, society in these two colonies had remained patrician, though neighbourly, and its attitude to democratic assertions had been coloured by memories of convict labour.

In north and central Queensland, meanwhile, sugar-growers employing Polynesian labourers had gone near to setting up a plantation society based on semi-slave labour. That break in the uniformity of Australian life was already being bridged before the end of the century by the breaking-up of large plantations and by the determination to end the Kanaka traffic; for the planters had not succeeded in their campaign for separation from Queensland, and democratic assumptions held the balance in the parliament in Brisbane as they did in Sydney or Melbourne.

In no question did the common assumptions of colonial society appear so stronly as in the exclusion of Chinese and other Asian immigrants. In this matter, despite the momentary waverings of colonies with large and undeveloped tropical areas, there was eventually an approach to unanimity between the colonies and between all classes. Many motives, both rational and merely prejudiced, entered into their desire to keep out Asian immigrants; but two were always mentioned—the desire to prevent 'the fair and reasonable' standard of living from being undermined by cheap labour, and the desire to preserve the homogeneity of colonial life. No other aspiration, declared Deakin, so wrought for federation as 'the desire that we should be one people, and remain one people without the admixture of other races'. One of the first actions of the federated commonwealth was the enactment of the White Australia Policy in the Immigration Restrictions Bill of 1901. White Australia was the negative expression of what had become an axiom of Australian political life, that this country should provide equality of opportunity and a fair and reasonable standard of living for all its citizens.

E

9

THE AUSTRALIAN LEGEND

By the end of the century, the Australian colonies had worked out a way of life that was in essentials the same over the whole continent. Its assumptions of democratic independence and equality of consideration might often be at war with economic and social facts; but there was no unquestioning acceptance of hierarchy, of one's station and its duties. Around the turn of the century, these attitudes were made part of the currency of common belief by a self-consciously Australian generation of writers, painters and cartoonists, and especially by the men who wrote and drew for the *Bulletin*.

In their work the outlines were fixed of an Australian legend or national myth. The flattering elements in this self-picture need to be countered by the sometimes dyspeptic remarks of those who have observed us from outside, as when Trollope, who liked us well enough, observed that Australia was like a young whale that had risen at last from the depths and was beginning to blow. Yet our imagination of ourselves may have its own truth; for it enshrines the things we believe in, the things that in general we want to be. It must also be said, however, that Australia today is different in important respects from the Australia of 1900, and the legend so universally accepted has now an even more tenuous relation with reality.

This legend was in part built up of observation of the land itself, in its varying moods, as the scene of a recognizably Australian life. Immigrants of an earlier day had not always found it monotonous and melancholy, as is sometimes supposed; but one of them, Marcus Clarke, author of *For the Term of His Natural Life* (1874), had turned his sense of its 'weird melancholy' into a literary convention.

A poem like 'L'Allegro' could never be written by an Australian. It is too airy, too sweet, too freshly happy. The Australian mountain forests are funereal, secret, stern. Their solitude is desolation. They seem to stifle, in their black gorges, a story of sullen despair. No tender sentiment is nourished in their shade. . . . All is fear-inspiring and gloomy. No bright fancies are linked with the memories of the mountains. Hopeless explorers have named them out of their sufferings—Mount Misery, Mount Dreadful, Mount Despair. . . . But the dweller in the wilderness acknowledges the subtle charm of this fantastic land of monstrosities . . . and the poet of our desolation begins to comprehend why free Esau loved his heritage of desert sand better than all the bountiful richness of Egypt.

An increasing proportion, however, of those who lived in Australia in the closing years of the century had been born here and had no sense of exile, no memories of the lush green of English trees and the trim neatness of park and farm to support such a mood. The native-born in Victoria increased from 62 per cent of its population in 1881, to close on 70 per cent in 1891, and to close on 80 per cent in 1901. To them the land was not something alien to which adjustment need be made; it was simply the familiar setting in which they had grown up. As they peopled it with their experiences and their memories, the weirdness, the silence and the melancholy which the newcomer often found in it when thoughts of his exile crowded in on him, ceased to be. If they noticed it at all, their eyes were able to see it even in its harshest moods with affection and occasionally with perception of its beauty.

Sometimes it took the newcomer to jolt the native out of mere acceptance into perception. It was the Swiss painter, Louis Buvelot, who first taught Australian painters to see their own landscape and to paint it with understanding. Such facts were obscured towards the end of the century when an aggressive assertion of the natural beauties of Australia became part of a self-conscious nationalism.

The Australian-born literary critic, A. G. Stephens of the *Bulletin,* took Marcus Clarke as the type of Englishman whose alien eyes could not see the native beauty.

Verlaine's cult of faded things, extolling the hinted hue before the gross colour, finds a natural home in Australia—in many aspects a land of faded things—of delicate purples, delicious greys, and dull, dreamy olives and ochres. Yet we have been content to let strangers foist upon us the English ideals of glaring green or staring red and orange; we have permitted them to denounce our grave harmonies of rock and vegetation, with shadow laid on tender shadow, light on dusky light. . . . Englishman Marcus Clarke has even called our gum-tree 'melancholy', our forests 'funereal'. . . . The grotesque English prejudice against things Australian, founded on no better reason than that they are unlike English things, still remains to vitiate the local sense of local beauty.

That passage was written in the first year of the commonwealth, formed by the federation of the six colonies in 1901; and its aggressive Australianism might seem merely to echo the celebrations of that time, were it not possible to parallel it much earlier. Indeed, Australian nationalism was more usual in this militant form in the nineteenth century than it has been in this. In his *Political Economy in Australia*, Professor La Nauze comments that David Syme's anti-English feeling was in harmony with contemporary radical ideas, and illustrates it from one of Syme's leaders in the Melbourne *Age*, 24 February 1860: 'Let us beware of being bled to death like Ireland—of being any longer phlebotomized to fill the pockets of an oligarchy which treads down Englishmen as it does Irishmen when they stand in its way.'

Local nationalism ranged widely from mild protest at failures of the British Government to consider colonial interests to serious discussions of republican independence of the colonies. The quality of protest died away in the first half of this century, as the irritants of imperial control disappeared, and as partnership in war bred a newer and stronger feeling of kinship and common interest.

While it lasted, however, one of the manifestations of colonial nationalism was a declaration of independence from the mould of European culture.

The University [wrote the *Bulletin* in 1887], in its absurd reverence for the extrinsic and the foreign, goes outside the literature, the language, the life and the history of its own country to seek for specious inspiration in a museum of antiquities, to burrow for worthless curiosities in the ruined catacombs and dusty cromlechs, which doubtless owed their origin to giants, but to giants of a long-forgotten epoch.

There is ignorance and absurdity in this, and the *Bulletin* outgrew it, drawing on the main stream of European literature as well as on the local scene. But in its time and place, that passage merely exaggerated an attitude that was spreading and had some value. Before Australia could create an intellectual and artistic culture that was not merely imitative, there had to be a blending on equal terms of its European heritage and colonial experience; and that could not occur while educated people assumed, as they so commonly did, that colonial life was merely crude and no fit source of artistic inspiration.

Beating against the neglect of their work which was bred by that assumption, those who sought inspiration in Australia and its life were naturally self-conscious in their nationalism and exaggerated in their attacks on those who aped the fashions of the old world. Self-consciousness and exaggeration sometimes limited the artistic stature of their work and left it to a later generation of writers to assume the Australian scene without flaunting it. But at this sacrifice they made room for the inspiration of Australian life, and in doing so they made popular an imagination of it which not all the changes of the twentieth century have been able to efface.

It was an Australian legend rather than a Victorian or West Australian or Queensland legend; for the colonies were at root alike in the manner of life that was lived in them and in their general attachment to the assumptions of a democratic egalitarian society.

It was shaped by none so much as by J. F. Archibald and A. G. Stephens of the Sydney *Bulletin* and by those who wrote for them, including many of their readers. The *Bulletin* in its youth was exuberant, radical and on principle irreverent. Its prejudices were many and strong. It was from time to time anti-royalty, anti-Jew, anti-squatter, anti-wowser (a term invented at the end of the century to describe a narrow-minded type of self-appointed Puritan censor); and if it was also anti-jingo, its own nationalism was not always so far from a local jingoism.

But it had saving graces. It encouraged its readers to write for it and provided a forum for those who were discovering literary and artistic inspiration in the Australian scene. Its Red Page applied standards of literary criticism which helped to improve the quality of Australian writing. Archibald, as Vance Palmer has written in his *National Portraits*, wanted 'to found a national newspaper. He had a passion to make his fellow-Australians aware of their country, aware of its varied life and individual character; he was eager to see the imitative habit of mind that was stultifying social life in the towns supplanted by the tough, sardonic independence that he felt was the spirit of the inland'.

Turning away from what he felt to be the smug and imitative life of the city, 'limping in apish imitation after London ideas, habits, and manners,' Archibald sought the native spirit of Australia in the bush. 'Nature', continues Vance Palmer, 'was a harsh mother whose whimsies had to be faced with stoicism. There was always a drought to be endured, a flood to be evaded, a pest to be fought. . . . It was no idyllic Australia these writers pictured under Archibald's guidance, but a gaunt, haggard continent that somehow evoked a natural loyalty in the people it bred.' The country and the things that happened in it were viewed through the eyes of the underdog, the swagman, the shearer and the drover rather than the squatter.

The Australian legend has been predominantly a bush legend, and not only because of Archibald's lead. Despite the increasing proportion of city dwellers, it is perhaps only now that any large

proportion of even urban Australians has no association through
relatives or early experience with the country. Tram-lines might be
more familiar to them than bush tracks, but it was natural when you
lived in the town to romanticize the country, particularly if you had
left your youth in it. The idea of a full and satisfying urban life is
only now taking root, and the sense of the country as escape from
the town, and as in some way more truly Australian, has not died.
So the cities still lack many of the amenities of urban gregariousness
that grace the older cities of Europe, while the old bush jingle still
has a power to move the Australian townsman that he could not
explain to his European counterpart:

> Stringy bark will light your fire,
> Green hide will never fail yer,
> Stringy bark and green hide
> Are the mainstay of Australia.

In imagination, at least, he still finds in the country a sense of
space and of release from the restrictions, the conventions and the
routine of the town.

It was J. Le Gay Brereton, city-bred friend and contemporary of
the greatest of the *Bulletin* writers, Henry Lawson, who wrote of a
city street:

> Clearly I saw men scurrying on the hour,
>   Young girls who weary all day on dainty feet,
>   Dandies whose socks betoken infinite pains,
> The life that springs and withers like a flower.
>   I heard the gangs go clanking down the street,
>   Intolerably patient of their chains.

The theme continues in Australian writing, and has been given
perhaps its best expression in Judith Wright's poem, 'Remittance
Man'.

> The spendthrift, disinherited and graceless,
> accepted his pittance with an easy air,
> only surprised he could escape so simply
> from the pheasant-shooting and the aunts in the close;
> took to the life, dropped easily out of knowledge,
> and tramping the backtracks in the summer haze
> let everything but life slip through his fingers.
>
> Blue blowing smoke of twigs from the noon fire,
> red blowing dust of roads where the teams go slow,
> sparse swinging shadow of trees no longer foreign

silted the memory of a greener climate.
The crazy tales, the hatters' crazy secrets,
the blind-drunk sprees indifferently forgiven,
and past them all, the track to escape and nowhere
suited his book, the freak who could never settle.

That pale stalk of a wench at the county ball
sank back forgotten in black mary's eyes,
and past the sallow circle of the plains' horizon
faded the rainy elms seen through the nursery window.

That harsh biblical country of the scapegoat
closed its magnificence finally round his bones
polished by diligent ants. The squire his brother,
presuming death, sighed over the documents,
and lifting his eyes across the inherited garden
let a vague pity blur the formal roses.

In the writings which have formulated this tradition, the quality of personal character held up for admiration is independence irrespective of station, and it is assumed that in Australia, at least, caste should have no place:

Let the word: Australian
Dignify the lowliest man.

In the Federal Convention Debates of 1897, Alfred Deakin replied to a member who wished to give greater powers to the Senate or upper house of parliament to control the lower, 'I will say that a gentleman who in Australia, in the nineteenth century, deplores the loss of the personal power of the English monarchy and of the English lords, as compared with the power of the Commons, is to my mind an anachronism'.

The positive aspect of the democratic assumption of natural equality is respect for character, wherever it appears. Its negative aspect was suspicion of any form of pretension that seemed to rest on older and more conservative traditions, or to hint at any ambition to set oneself up as superior to one's fellows. Indeed, there was a hallowed tradition of distrust of wealth and honours, as likely, unless disproof were offered, to have been discreditably gained.

When they pin the Stars and Garters, when they write the titles rare,
The men who earned the honours are the men who won't be there.

Dr Russel Ward in *The Australian Legend* argues that the combination of loyalty to one's fellows with disrespect towards superior orders may be traced back to the convicts. It was a combination inherent in their situation and passed on by convict old-hands to the new-chum immigrants who learned attitudes as well as bush-craft from them. Towards the end of the century, he argues, this bush ethos captured the Australian labour movement through the influence of the bush unions and was turned virtually into a national creed by the *Bulletin* writers who turned to the outback and the bush unions for themes and inspirations. The argument is appealing although unprovable. Apart from some understatement of the degree to which the deference for rank survived, it may too much neglect other and more urban sources of loyalty to equals and resentment of superiors. Migration itself may well have weakened acceptance of traditional social rank while making working class immigrants even in towns look to each other for protection from loneliness and disaster.

It is a tradition that can be good or bad. It can make for recognition of individual worth apart from status, and for the corrective touch of cynicism that an imperfect world requires. It has also made for a failure to value exceptional qualities. Mr H. M. Green, historian of Australian literature, has commented, 'Australian conditions encourage fellowship rather than leadership; the atmosphere is unfavourable to the growth of "tall poppies", and encourages talent rather than genius'.

That statement may be argued; but 'mateship' has been the most widely discussed element in our tradition. It appeared early, for it was noticed that ex-convict bush workers stood by each other to a degree that was thought worthy of remark. Not that this trait is to be traced simply to the fellowship of convicts in adversity; it was nourished throughout our colonial history by circumstances and necessity. So often lacking such amenities as doctors and hospitals, colonists were compelled to turn to each other, and the habit has persisted.

The writers who have outlined our picture of ourselves have given this mutual help the special twist of continuing loyalty to one's mate whether he deserves it or not, simply because he is one's mate. Vance Palmer has stated the theme most clearly in his short story, 'The Cook's Mate' (in *Separate Lives*). The cook's mate has been given a job at a water-drilling camp, though he proves useless, simply because he is the cook's mate and the cook is popular. As the job nears its end, the cook's mate disappears, and with him £13. The boss proposes to put the mounted police on his tracks.

The cook's red face showed genuine signs of distress. He was getting his blankets together and rolling them into a swag. 'No, don't do that, Boss,' he pleaded. 'For God's sake keep it quiet. It's up to me to stand the racket and I don't mind. Shorty's a bit twisted in the grain but he's not a bad sort when you come to know him. And then he's a mate of mine. . . . Don't tell the boys, but we done time together once in St Helena, after the big strike. Shed-burning business it was. That's God knows how many years ago, but Shorty's never been able to run straight since, somehow. I'll catch him up at Johnny's shanty, and I'll belt hell out of him before he's too drunk to put up his hands. This ain't the first time he's done it on me —no, nor the fourth—but a man's got to stick to his mate and see him through. . . . You take it out of my cheque, and I'll take it out of him.' And reaching his bridle from the nail, with the air of a man shouldering a burden that had been allotted to him from the beginning, he went resign-edly after his horse.

The essence of the tradition is loyalty to one's fellows, and the strength of its appeal may be seen in the restraining power of the term 'scab' in an Australian union. In the loneliness of the bush, loyalty might go beyond one's human companions, as in Henry Lawson's story 'That There Dog o' Mine' in *While the Billy Boils*. 'That there dog', said Macquarie the shearer, 'is a better dog than I'm a man . . . and a better Christian. He's been a better mate to me than I ever was to any man—or any man to me.'

The years at the turn of the century when the theme of mateship was most exploited in Australian writing were years of drought culminating in the desolation of 1902. The hardships of those years, added to the normal trials of life in the outback, bred a special admir-ation for the grit and cheerful endurance which were simple necessities of pioneering. With these qualities in the Australian legend is connected a more aggressive gambling quality, a readiness 'to have a go at a thing', 'a willingness', writes Mr H. M. Green, 'to take a risk with things, and a determination to see them through'.

These attitudes fused with the traditional disrespect for human pretentiousness in a native and cynical brand of humour, often disrespectful, often profane, and often grim. As it is expressed in a flavour, a turn of words, a twist to a story, or a distinctive Australian school of cartoonists, it cannot be readily illustrated here. It could not defeat an equally persistent romanticism; and, indeed, it required a race of romantics to retain their affection for the drought-stricken country of those years.

In William Lane's newspaper *The Boomerang* and in his writings in *The Worker* in the 'eighties and 'nineties, romanticism took the form of a Utopian fervour which, in its extreme naïveté, was ephem-eral. But the assumption has been persistent, through all the common-placeness of livelihood and politics, that this last-discovered continent need not be fettered to the inequalities and injustices of the old world.

She is committed [wrote Furphy in *Such is Life*] to no usages of petrified injustice; she is clogged by no fealty to shadowy idols, enshrined by ignorance, and upheld by misplaced homage alone; she is cursed by no memories of fanaticism and persecution; she is innocent of hereditary national jealousy, and free from the envy of sister states.

In fact, neither Australia nor Australians were a *tabula rasa* on which a new message to the world could be written without fetter from the old. Participating in the industrialization of the world, Australians could not, and cannot, escape its problems. But the assumption that old restrictions on individual independence have no natural right here has been a persistent element in Australian attitudes. In a country that has of necessity greatly relied on government action, it is nevertheless true that the essence of Australian democracy has been a belief in the rights of the individual, without thought of status. The very demand for state action has in some part sprung from this belief—to secure equality of opportunity, a fair and reasonable livelihood, political rights. The call for state intervention in Australian democracy has often been, in short, an expression of its individualism.

The Australian legend is not necessarily a picture of the Australians; but it is a picture of ideals that have been dominant in Australia, and ideals may at least take part in moulding character. Indeed, the best summary of the Australian tradition may well be Dr C. W. Bean's carefully documented account, in *The Australian Imperial Force in France During the Allied Offensive,* of the Australian diggers in France in 1918:

Yet at heart even the oldest Australian soldier was incorrigibly civilian. However thoroughly he accepted the rigid army methods as conditions temporarily necessary, he never became reconciled to continuous obedience to orders, existence by rule, and lack of privacy. His individualism had been so strongly implanted as to stand out after years of subordination. Even on the Western Front he had exercised his vote in the Australian elections and in the referendums as to conscription, and it was largely through his own act in these ballots that the Australian people had rejected conscription and that, to the end, the AIF consisted entirely of volunteers. He was subject to no death penalty for disobedience or failure to face the enemy. . . . In Australia the distinction into social classes was so resented that it was difficult to get born Australians to serve as officers' batmen and grooms, who by the English tradition were servants. . . .

He was accustomed to take decisions, and was always ready to run risks for an object in which he was interested—whether the saving of a mate, the securing of a souvenir, or an unlicensed trip to Paris (or, after the war, to Cologne). He was less affected than most men by risk of punishment, but was bound to his fellows, and to the Old Country and the Allies, by a tense bond of democratic loyalty—a man must 'stand by his mates' at all costs; and as he knew only one social horizon, that of race, most of his officers came within that category. He was the easiest man in the world to interest and lead, but was intolerant of incompetent or uninteresting leaders. . . .

Except for a few demonic spirits one immersion in a great battle more than satisfied the eagerness that had led many to enlist, and left in almost all minds an often sub-conscious but never-absent dread. Most Australians yearned for return to their country with an intensity of longing of which they had not believed themselves capable, but which was remarked by most other soldiers who met them.

The Australian legend of the turn of the century asserted those qualities which seemed most distinctive, and they were the qualities most easily associated with 'the nomad tribe' of bush-workers. Whatever may be said of the truth of that legend at the turn of the century or at the time of Gallipoli, it is no longer found to satisfy the need of Australians in the highly industrialized and still more urbanized country of today for an imagination of themselves which may support and inspire them.

The contemporary debate on Australians and their values will be a subject for the concluding chapter.

IO

THE COMMONWEALTH

Nevertheless the bush legend has maintained its hold on the Australian imagination. We still refer to 'the real, typical Australians outside the capital cities'; the phrase is taken from a Melbourne newspaper of 1950, and variations of the theme recur daily. In fact, Australians outside the capital cities are today less representative of the Australian community as a whole than the majority who are city dwellers. Simply, their manner of life is more distinctive in being further removed from European patterns.

For the twentieth century has seen great changes in the community which created that legend. The number of Australians who live, not in the bush but in towns, has increased from roughly one-third to over four-fifths; and of these town dwellers, almost three-quarters live in the six capital cities of the commonwealth. In terms of value, Australians make more in urban factories than they grow on farms and sheep-runs and dig in mines although mining is growing fast. Australia still has its frontier areas; but they loom larger in the imaginative picture of the country than in its economy. In short, the structure of the Australian economy and of Australian society has been growing nearer to the pattern of the older industrial countries of the world.

Yet it is not merely as a literary convention that the aspirations of the bush legend continue. In large measure it still symbolizes the social attitudes and the most widely accepted political ideals of the community. The belief in independence and equality of title to consideration lives on, together with the belief that a new country should be more readily able to bend economic law to its service in providing 'a fair deal all round'. The interest of the last sixty years is the adaptation to new circumstances of those colonial aspirations as the conditions which bred them have receded into history.

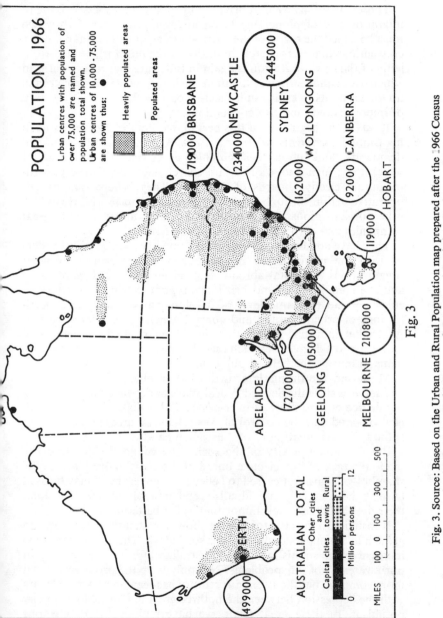

POPULATION 1966

Urban centres with population of over 75,000 are named and population total shown.
Urban centres of 10,000 - 75,000 are shown thus: ●

Heavily populated areas

Populated areas

2445000 SYDNEY

719000 BRISBANE

234000 NEWCASTLE

162000 WOLLONGONG

92000 CANBERRA

119000 HOBART

2108000 MELBOURNE

105000 GEELONG

727000 ADELAIDE

499000 PERTH

AUSTRALIAN TOTAL

Capital cities   Other cities and towns   Rural

0   Million persons   12

MILES   100   0   100   300   500

Fig. 3

Fig. 3. Source: Based on the Urban and Rural Population map prepared after the 1966 Census by the Commonwealth Bureau of Census and Statistics, Canberra, 1967.

Those conditions were in brief the uprooting and social mixing of migration and of pioneering in an undeveloped country, to which must be added the revolt of the native-born against social and literary conventions that were merely imitative of the old world and patronizing of the new. Migration is again in full spate, but to a country in which rural pioneering is a minor incident; while the Australian no longer needs to establish his self-respect by flaunting his defiance of imported and imitative conventions.

It was at the beginning of this period that Pember Reeves wrote in his *State Experiments in Australia and New Zealand* that colonial democrats 'look upon their colonies as co-operative societies of which they, men and women, are shareholders, while the governments are elective boards of directors. They believe that by co-operative action through the State they can compete with trusts and other organizations of capital abroad, and dispense with great companies and corporations within their borders'.

They have not dispensed with great companies within their borders or with the participation in their economic enterprise of great organizations of capital abroad. Nor, given their small population and the complexity of modern industry, could they have achieved efficiency and the same level of development without the concentrations of private capital and control which mark a large part of Australian industry, unless they had been ready to accept state enterprise to a degree for which there has been no consistent majority demand outside the field of public utilities.

Moreover, the dramatic growth of Australian mining, industry, and services since the Second World War has depended to an increasing degree on an inflow of overseas capital which, while welcomed, is also feared, lest the control of Australian resources and enterprise should slip too greatly out of Australian hands.

But if the complexity of the social and economic structure has made the task of 'the elective board of directors' more difficult, the shareholders have not ceased to believe that government may be used to serve the essentially individualistic end of preserving their freedom, their livelihood and their opportunities for betterment.

It would be a mistake to suppose, however, that there has been no growth in the understanding of this social task. There has been some increase in the sophistication of Australian life, some deepening in our awareness of our problems. Not only have the problems grown more complex, but the twentieth century has seen, in two world wars with the depression between them, three great hammer-blows to any optimism. In these great trials, we have realized more fully our participation in the common fate of man, that we could not completely escape either history or the world. Korea and Vietnam have confirmed the lesson.

The debates of the first parliament of the Commonwealth of Australia fill seventeen fat volumes of Hansard. The greatest of those debates was that on the Immigration Restriction Bill. In the course of it, Henry Bourne Higgins, whose stature will grow and not wither with time, quoted Froude's *Oceana*:

We have our national concerns to look after and our national risks to run, and therefore our thoughts and anxieties are enlarged. They [the Australians] have none of those interests; their situation does not allow it. They will have good lawyers among them, good doctors, good men of science, engineers, merchants, manufacturers, as the Romans had in the decline of the Empire. But of the heroic type of man, of whom poets will sing and after ages be anxious to read, there will not be so many, when the generation is gone which was born and bred in the old world. Such men are not wanted, and would have no work cut out for them.

When Higgins quoted that passage in 1901, there was much to support its argument, as there had been when Froude wrote it in 1886. The new commonwealth, like the old colonies, was still secured by British sea-power; and the utilitarian job of developing the potential resources of the land seemed on the whole to call for perseverance and practical common sense rather than heroic qualities as Froude understood them.

Yet the colonies had already produced men of exceptional stature like Alfred Deakin, and that genuine idealism—the belief in the possibilities of Australia, not only for wealth but for a more widely distributed freedom—acted as a spur both to the native-born like Deakin and to the immigrant like Higgins. Limited and utilitarian as colonial life commonly was, such men as Deakin and Higgins were not men of limited mind and limited intention; and for them the material task of securing livelihood and opportunity to the people at large was merely a prerequisite to the setting free of energies for the mental and moral growth they hoped would follow. Whether later days have produced men of their stature or not, there is no doubt that the twentieth century has had work in plenty 'cut out for them'.

The vigorous experimental quality of colonial democracy was never more confidently in control than in the years which followed the formation of the commonwealth, and continued, a halcyon period, up to the outbreak of war in 1914. The liberals had in large part recovered from their hesitations of the depression years and, under the inspiration of such men as Alfred Deakin, were evolving a programme of social democracy which differed only in degree and temper from that of the young and vigorous Labour Party.

It is true that the political life of the commonwealth began in great confusion; for the federal arena had attracted the rival talents of the various colonies, and their individual rivalries were more evident than grouping according to principle or programme during the first few years. Within a decade, when the fiscal issue was settled in 1908 by the commonwealth's adoption of protection, that grouping was to take the form of a fusion of non-labour parties opposed to the rapidly growing Labour Party; but only after Deakin's Liberals, held in office by labour support, had carried out much of the programme on which both liberals and labour were agreed.

George Reid might stalk up and down the electoral jungle, loudly proclaiming the presence of a 'socialist tiger' and seeking the electors' support for himself as its hunter; but, after all, as premier of New South Wales he had been responsible but a few years earlier for legislation branded with the same stripes. The majority of electors were not convinced, and preferred those liberals and labour men who would go on from political to social democracy.

The type of this liberalism was Deakin's 'New Protection' policy, itself in tune with the ideas of some labour men.

'The "old" protection', he said, 'contented itself with making good wages possible. The "new" protection seeks to make them actual.' He imposed excise duties on agricultural machinery, with the provision that manufacturers should be exempted from payment of these duties if it could be shown that they were paying fair and reasonable wages; and he foreshadowed the application of this policy to protected local industry in general. The legislation was disallowed by the High Court, but its principle of the 'fair and reasonable' wage was adopted by Mr Justice Higgins of the Commonwealth Court of Conciliation and Arbitration in his 'harvester judgment'.

The principle of compulsory arbitration in industrial disputes, whether by courts of law or wages boards, had been accepted in New Zealand and the Australian colonies during the 'nineties. The commonwealth court was established in 1904 to deal with disputes extending beyond the borders of one state. It was for long handicapped by its limitation to such disputes and by its inability to declare a common rule for an industry as a whole. But these limitations have largely disappeared in practice as industries and unions have spilled over state boundaries. Even where a dispute cannot be treated as interstate, the arbitration courts and wages boards of the separate states have in large part come to accept the decisions of the federal court as a guide to their own decisions.

The Commonwealth Court of Conciliation and Arbitration, now the Commonwealth Conciliation and Arbitration Commission, has, therefore, come to be a body of great importance in the economic life of the country; and, indeed, its determination of hours and wages make it in effect one of the important institutions of economic planning. The first steps in its rise to prestige and power were taken by Henry Bourne Higgins when he was appointed President of the Court in 1906. He brought to its work two conceptions, that the rule of law might be extended to industrial conflicts, and that it should be law with a positive content of social justice.

In 1907 Higgins was required under the new protection legislation to determine whether the wages paid by H. V. McKay's harvester factory were 'fair and reasonable'. It was not a question which could be or was expected to be decided by legal doctrine or precedent, and Higgins's inquiry was a significant foretaste of the future development of the court as a body trying by common-sense means to work out a reasonable solution along the lines of natural justice and national interest.

It was in this judgment that Higgins established the principle of 'a basic wage' based on 'the normal needs of the average employee, regarded as a human being living in a civilized community'. This, he wrote later in his *New Province for Law and Order,*

was to be the primary test in ascertaining the minimum wage that would be treated as 'fair and reasonable' in the case of unskilled labourers. . . . Treating marriage as the usual fate of adult men, a wage which does not allow of the matrimonial condition and the maintenance of about five persons in a home would not be treated as a living wage. As for the secondary wage, it seemed to be the safest course, for an arbitrator not initiated into the mysteries of the several crafts, to follow the distinctions in grade between employees as expressed for many years.

Until the depression in 1931 tempered it by consideration of industry's capacity to pay, the requirement that the minimum wage should satisfy 'the normal needs of the average employee regarded as a human being living in a civilized community' controlled the awards of both federal and state wage-fixing bodies, and in general Higgins's harvester judgment was taken as the basis of calculation. In short, economic considerations must wait on a certain minimum of social justice. Higgins wrote:

Men are willing enough to work, but even good work does not necessarily insure a proper human subsistence, and when they protest against
this condition of things they are told that their aims are too 'materialistic'.
Give them relief from their materialistic anxiety, give them reasonable
certainty that their essential needs will be met by honest work, and you
release infinite stores of human energy for higher efforts, for nobler
ideals, when 'Body gets its sop, and holds its noise, and leaves soul free a
little'.

The experience that greater security and leisure have not always
been used for higher efforts has not disproved this faith, though it
has demonstrated that a good use of leisure required both facilities and
guidance, and that we have scarcely begun to understand the problems of leisure. For, if poverty has not been eliminated, affluence
has grown and has brought its own problems, of which juvenile
delinquency is only the most obvious.

Ten years after federation, the lead in shaping Australian democracy passed from Deakin's Liberals to the Labour Party. Its rise to
power had been so rapid as to surprise its own supporters, and it had
held office as the Government of the Commonwealth for two short
periods before its return for a longer session in 1910.

The Labour Party shocked members of the older parties less by its
programme than by its discipline. It was, of course, no new thing for
a member to represent a sectional interest rather than the nation; but
the Labour Party, though it sought middle-class support with a
programme of studied moderation, was frankly a party to serve the
working classes.

Before it could hope to win enough seats to govern, it could exact
some of its programme from one or other of the older parties as
concession in return for support. That power was lost when labour
members were split by the same issue of free trade versus protection
which divided the other parties. Out of such experience was evolved
the caucus, the meeting of all labour members, and the 'pledge' to
vote as caucus decided. The older parties had been marked by their
lack of discipline, the ease with which they broke up and regrouped
on different issues or about different leaders. To that almost anarchic
freedom, labour's discipline was at first abhorrent; a generation's
experience has replaced abhorrence with a discipline less complete
but not radically different from labour's.

Labour's programme in the 1910–13 session was no different in
principle from Deakin's. It established the Commonwealth Bank,
rather mildly taxed unimproved land values (with the object of
breaking up large estates and with the effect, at least, of increasing
revenue), liberalized the old-age pension scheme brought in by

Deakin's Government in 1909, and enacted invalid pensions and maternity allowances. It was all in keeping with the traditional distrust of monopoly, by no means confined to the Labour Party, and the traditional belief in using the State to equalize the opportunities of a fair and reasonable livelihood. It contained no programme of root-and-branch reconstruction.

Labour agreed also with the policy of preceding governments in a nationalistic approach to the defence of Australia. Its establishment of an Australian Navy in preference to contributing towards the British Navy was the fulfilment of Deakin's policy; and if it was labour which first advocated and finally completed the system of universal and compulsory military training, this was the policy of all parties. It was Deakin who in 1907 had described the general preference for 'a citizen soldiery inspired by patriotism' over a standing professional army. But for labour this was universal training for service in Australia and for the defence of Australia. The old anti-imperial note was in diminuendo; but labour still retained the suspicion, quickened by the Boer War, of imperialistic adventures.

Into the sunny atmosphere of prosperity and mild, if heatedly debated, reforms, there burst the storm of war. For most Australians, Balkan and Bosnian clouds were far below the horizon and the storm burst for them from a clear sky. Some had seen further. The symbolism of *The Wanderer* written some time earlier by Christopher Brennan, perhaps the greatest, certainly the least parochial, of Australian poets, prefigures the whirling of the winds of war into the calm of sheltered nation building which had been so free of disturbing experience and of disturbing profundities.

Ye have built you unmysterious homes and ways in the wood
where of old ye went with sudden eyes to the right and left;
and your going was now made safe and your staying comforted,
for the forest edge itself, holding old savagery
in unsearch'd glooms, was your houses' friendly barrier.
And now that the year goes winterward, ye thought to hide
behind your gleaming panes, and where the hearth sings merrily
make cheer with meat and wine, and sleep in the long night,
and the uncared wastes might be a crying unhappiness.
But I, who have come from the outer night, I say to you the winds are up
and terribly will they shake the dry wood:
the woods shall awake, hearing them, shall awake to be toss'd and riven,
and make a cry and a parting in your sleep all night
as the wither'd leaves go whirling all night along all ways.
And when ye come forth at dawn, uncomforted by sleep,
ye shall stand at amaze, beholding all the ways overhidden

with worthless drift of the dead and all your broken world:
and ye shall not know whence the winds have come, nor shall ye know
whither the yesterdays have fled, or if they were.

It has been common rhetoric that Australia became a nation on
Gallipoli. The statement is true in a sense, but not for the reasons
commonly given. The heroism of the Anzacs was not different in
kind from the courage and endurance of the early pioneers. Australia
became a nation because for the first time she was plunged into the
responsibilities of nationhood.

Froude had commented in 1886 that colonial circumstances called
for talent rather than greatness. The First World War was the first
public occasion which required of large numbers of Australians in
common with men of many countries that they should rise above
their average selves. How they did so is known history and needs no
repetition here. Pride in their deeds could not be all, and at least for
some people the slaughter and the accompaniment at home of civil
strife and divided counsels stirred both perception and conscience
deeper. Henceforth, through all the rhetoric of public statements,
there is some increase in realism, in a sense of difficulties and
responsibilities.

Australia was not so fully involved as in the last war, nor did the
battles come so close home. Yet the price it paid for the glory that its
men undoubtedly earned was heavy; 60,000 of them died, a heavy
loss for its small population, while at home the strains of war brought
more serious rifts into the community than it had known before.

The later years of war forced a rapid growth of Australian industry.
Already by 1891, industrial workers had grown as numerous as rural
workers, though the depression of the 'nineties reversed the trend for
a time. Most industries were still very small and very domestic in the
goods they made—shoes and clothing, processed foods and beer, as
well as farm implements and gas for light and power. But there were
considerable concentrations of workmen in the railways and tram-
ways, on the wharves, and in coal-mining and mining for base metals;
while heavy industry was already growing strongly before 1914 as a
product of mining. Its growth was hastened by the requirements of
war.

Small iron-foundries had been set up early in the history of the
colonies; but the history of the iron and steel industry in Australia
entered a new phase with the building of a modern blast furnace at
Lithgow in New South Wales in 1905. This was soon surpassed when
in 1915 the Broken Hill Proprietary Company's steel works went into
production at Newcastle, centre of the northern coal-fields of New

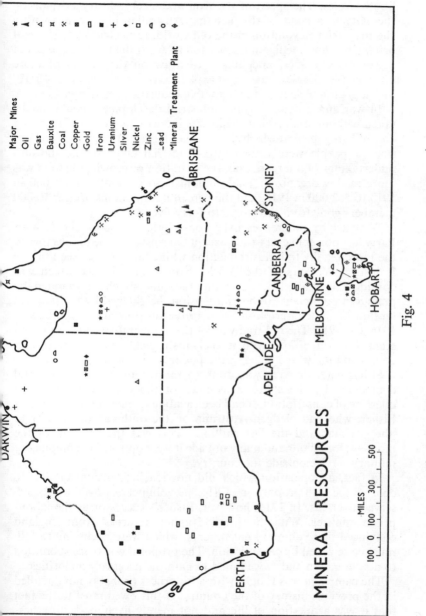

Fig. 4. Source: Based on a map of mineral resources in *The Reader's Digest Atlas of Australia*, 1968, Reader's Digest Association, Sydney

South Wales. The speed of the iron and steel industry's expansion thereafter is a mark of the fact that Australian history falls within the Industrial Revolution of the old world. It has had some share of originality; but intelligent adaptation to Australian circumstances of matured techniques, and ability to draw on the capital of more advanced economies, have most explained the rapid rise of the 'BHP' into a great, efficient and imaginative industrial enterprise.

In war and post-war years, industrial development could not be taken without strain. That strain was increased by the rapidly rising cost of living, behind which rising wages lagged. As a greater proportion of people were drawn into industrial employment and into undertakings of a larger scale, the irritation of growing distress was more readily organized. Trade unionists increased from 498,000 in 1913 to 582,000 in 1918, and the percentage in unions of over 10,000 members grew from thirty-five to forty-five.

Wrecked by differences over conscription in 1916, the Labour Party lost power in every state except Queensland. The unions turned the more readily to industrial action while the extremist section, the Industrial Workers of the World, gained an influence which was considerable, though it was temporary and much exaggerated by press and politicians. Industrial tension, heightened by the political tension of the conscription fight, broke out into bitter conflicts in 1916 and 1917. The old tradition of the co-operative commonwealth seemed at stake, and with it such instruments as the arbitration courts and the whole belief in the possible rule of law in industry.

Still greater damage was done to the tradition of experimental democracy by the splitting asunder of the community over the question of conscription. It had been a labour prime minister, Andrew Fisher, who had pledged Australia on the outbreak of the war to 'the last man and the last shilling'. This was the emotion of the moment, for labour and many outside it were opposed to compulsory military service outside the country.

In fact, a population which did not reach 5,000,000 until 1918 enlisted the high proportion of 416,809 volunteers, of whom 329,000 served overseas. In 1916, however, Fisher's successor as the labour prime minister, William Morris Hughes, returned from England convinced that voluntary enlistments, which were beginning to fall, must be replaced by conscription. The proposal was twice submitted to a referendum and twice failed to gain the necessary majorities.

The campaign was fought with a bitterness probably not equalled in the previous history of the country. If this owed most to the fact that it was a question of life and not merely livelihood, bitterness was added to it by all the strains of war, by industrial unrest, by the arbitrariness of the government which in the heat of conflict used its wartime powers with decreasing restraint, and by the aftermath of the Easter Rebellion in Dublin.

Almost a quarter of Australia's population is Irish in descent. Roman Catholic clergy and laity spoke on both sides of the conscription question, or made it clear that they regarded it as a matter of state and of individual judgment. But a considerable section of Australia's Irish population was moved by sympathy with the Sinn Fein into denunciations of Britain and the war and were in turn denounced by many of the non-Irish as traitors. This added bitterness to the contest without clearly affecting the result, for voting figures showed no correlation with the varying proportions of Roman Catholics, mainly of Irish descent, in the states.

Ireland's wrongs have ceased to ripple the Australian waters; but it was long before the bitter intolerance of the conscription struggle, raised to great heat by the Irish question, was forgotten. The legacy of that time was the destruction for a decade or more of that progressive, common-sense liberalism which had marked both liberal and labour parties to so great a degree.

When, after Hughes's first referendum, the labour caucus discussed a vote of no-confidence in his leadership, he and twenty-four members left the party, were supported in office for a time by their former opponents and eventually joined with them to form the Nationalist Party. The Labour Party, deprived of its leaders, lost in confidence and public appeal what it possibly gained in radicalism.

On the nationalist side, the accession of the former labour members brought no marked addition of liberalism; for the strikes, the struggle with the IWW, the bitter personalities of the conscription campaign and the taste of wartime powers had undermined their liberalism and left hostility to the remnant of labour in the ascendant. The same fears and hostilities had weakened the liberalism that had marked a large section of the right-wing parties before the war. The sense of common objectives pursued at different rates and by different means gave way in many to an assumption of unbridgeable opposition.

Nor could Australia escape the letting down of hopes at the war's end and the tensions of the return from war to peace; 1919 surpassed 1917 in the extent of its industrial disputes. The deep divisions of the later war years persisted for a time and took on an ideological doctrinaire tone which reflected a world riven by revolutionary struggles and seemed to have little relation with the local experimental and non-doctrinal tradition of politics. 'The fumes of the ancient hells have invaded your spirit,' wrote Frank Wilmot, a poet always sensitive to the common feeling.

It is doubtful, however, whether there was any profound or enduring departure from the old piecemeal radicalism. As industrial monopolies grew both in size and in the proportion of Australian industry controlled by them, and as trade unions grew correspondingly, there was some sharpening of the sense of the conflicting interests of capital and labour. Despite a wider readiness, however, to interpret local problems in terms of the world's ideological divisions, the old piece-meal bargaining attitude remained generally in control, and in time the isolationist quality of Australian radicalism reasserted itself as awareness of international affairs died away before preoccupation with local concerns.

A decade of progress blurred, if it did not fully remove, the postwar unsettlement of spirit. But the course of material progress did not run smooth and prosperity was uneasily based. Unemployment remained at a consistently higher level than in the years before the war and caused much hostility towards the elaborate schemes of assisted immigration which were devised as part of the post-war settlement of the country. These schemes illustrated the economic unsoundness of a decade which in many ways justified the jeremiads of Australia's economists of that time. Actually, the number of immigrants fell far short of the unbased expectations of some politicians, while the results of plans to settle a number of these immigrants together with Australian returned soldiers on the land as small farmers showed once again the great complexity and difficulty of mass settlement.

Other factors apart, the prices paid for land in a time of inflated values were too high, and the blocks in many areas too small to return an adequate livelihood. Heavy debts were incurred to finance migration and closer settlement and the public works which settlement required—irrigation, roads and railways. Agricultural output was increased and a number of excellent farmers established by these schemes; but quickly the tale began of settlers abandoning their holdings, either because of inexperience or personal unsuitability to country life, or because no degree of experience and aptitude could have overcome the handicap of high costs, uncertain prices and inadequate blocks.

By 1937, when the depression had turned struggle into complete failure for many, proportions of assisted settlers, varying from 30 per cent in one state to close on 60 per cent in another, had left their holdings; and a large proportion of the money advanced to them had had to be written off.

In the context of the return of soldiers from the wars, the emphasis of these schemes had naturally been on settling large numbers of men on the land. That was an attitude proper to a pioneering community; but Australian farming was already passing out of its pioneering stage and the soldier settlement schemes were an anachronism. Increase of primary production now depended less on an increase in the number of farmers than on an increase of efficiency, by means of retreat from those marginal lands which could give an adequate return only in times of exceptional prices or exceptional seasons, and by means of a consolidation of farms into holdings large enough to make economical use of mechanical devices. In Victoria, despite the 5,000 soldier-settlers who remained on the land, the number of farmers is now much the same as in 1918, while the increased primary production of Australia as a whole comes from a smaller number of holdings, though from a larger area.

If returned soldiers and assisted immigrants were to provide the men, and heavy borrowing provided the money, the markets—third element in this triad of post-war settlement—were harder to find. It was difficult to keep the costs of production in Australian conditions within the purchasing power of populations in other countries, and Australian sugar, butter, dried fruits, and, in the depression years, wheat had to be heavily subsidized to compete at all in English markets.

Such subsidy was but one part of protection all round. The war had stimulated many industries, both small and great, which, when peace brought renewed competition from overseas, swelled the cry for higher protective tariffs. Protection did nurture local industry; and, as the Tariff Enquiry Committee of 1929 reported, 'the same average income for the *same population* could not have been obtained without protection'. But there were pitfalls in its path.

The cost to the Australian consumer of bounties and tariffs, estimated at £36,000,000 in that year, was not beyond the ability of Australian resources to meet; but some part of that burden did represent the failure of much local industry to lower its costs by improved efficiency. The greater readiness to seek higher protection than lower production costs was an essential point of ill-health in the economic enterprise of the time.

The uneasy spiral of the 'twenties rose rapidly—higher duties, higher costs of living, demands for higher wages, demands for still higher protection to cover rising wage-bills. High protection caused particular discontent in the more rural states, such as Western Australia which complained that it was being taxed for the good of eastern industrialists. Manufactures were an important element in the national output and national income; but they were still an insignificant part of Australian exports. Overseas credits, to meet interest payments on loans and to pay for imports, were gained almost entirely by the primary industries which made up 96 per cent of the value of exports in 1928. As many of these were subsidized, they earned overseas credits at the cost of higher prices to the Australian consumer.

The foundations were insecure; yet the appearance of prosperity was undoubted, reaching boom proportions in 1928. But it was a wretched decade, adding little but wealth to our possessions. The dullness of the 'twenties was a world-wide phenomenon and Australia shared in it. Reaction from the strains and heroics of war and the collapse of traditional standards contributed to its bankruptcy.

There were also local reasons. Not for seventy years had the Australian community been so divided as it was over conscription and the industrial strife of the war years. Its leaders lost to its opponents, political Labour wandered for a decade in the political wilderness. If that time was spent in reformulating its programme, its adoption of 'the socialist objective' in 1921 and memories of industrial strife scared away for some time to come the small group of swinging voters who determine the fate of political parties in Australia.

Those same experiences had left conservatism rather than the positive liberalism of Deakin's time in the ascendant among their opponents. The decade saw the political organization of rural interests, in the Country Party, an aspect of the competition of sectional interests for subsidy, tariff or other advantage which, always a major element in politics, was at that time held less in check by a shared attachment to national ideals than it had been in the opening years of the century.

If in business the decade was one of feverish activity, in other fields it was a time of decline, or at best of fallow. The experimental and reforming zeal which had marked public education in the first twenty years of the century, under the leadership of such men as Peter Board in New South Wales and Frank Tate in Victoria, died away, and, while primary and secondary education were choked with too much administrative control, public education at all levels was starved for a want of readiness to spend money on it.

In the arts, the picture is somewhat similar. The great rise of public interest in music had not begun. The architecture of the time was as regrettable as its fashions. Some good writing was done in the 'twenties; but it received no great interest or reward. Painting was in a stronger position; but, with the brilliant exception of Max Meldrum and his pupils and their pursuit of optical impressions, it was the continuation of established tradition rather than the exploration of new paths.

In the field of social legislation, so optimistically undertaken in the opening years of the century, little was done. Australians sometimes boasted, though somewhat languidly, of the country's role as a social laboratory; but, in many types of social service it lagged behind older countries such as England and Germany. National Insurance schemes had been proposed by the Cook Government in 1913 and by the Bruce-Page Government in 1923 but had petered out, first in the preoccupations of war and then in disputes as to whether national insurance should be financed only by the tax payer or from wages as well.

The weaknesses in the country's social services—only Queensland had a state system of unemployment relief—were probed when, in 1929–30, prosperity collapsed in the depression, a second great hammer-blow to traditional optimism. World prices of Australia's chief exports fell drastically. Although exports of primary products were greater in quantity in 1931–2 than in 1928–9, their value fell to little more than half. Meanwhile, the prices of imports fell more slowly, while the ability of the community to buy the goods and services it needed was still further reduced by the cessation of overseas loans and by the continuing burden of interest payments on the heavy overseas borrowing of the preceding years. The depression made clear Australia's economic vulnerability, her dependence, as a country of a small home market and incomplete development, on stable export prices and on loans.

If adversity calls out greatness, Australians in common with many other peoples were then in the way of greatness, when even registered unemployment rose to close on 30 per cent. In fact for many, and especially for the young, it meant frustration of promise. Doles and relief work miserably dragged out the time; and many unaccustomed feet trod the streets and the bush roads wearily and unsuccessfully seeking work. Frank Wilmot went to the heart of that experience in his poem, 'Upon a Row of Old Boots and Shoes in a Pawnbroker's Window':

> But I'm not weaving sentimental stories
> About these boots and their departed glories.
> Up to blue heaven my entreaty rises
> For food, for shelter, and not to pawn my shoes.

The depression put an end to the unquestioning optimism of the 'twenties, and brought more to listen to those economists who had questioned the health of Australian economic life and to those geographers who had explained the limits of its natural resources.

Above all, it laid stress on the problem of discovering a securer basis for the 'fair and reasonable' livelihood than it seemed we had discovered in the past. Meanwhile the shock and suffering of that time gained adherents for all the ideologies and lent a more pervasive tone of the doctrinaire to our political and industrial life than had marked it before, except, perhaps, during the First World War.

There were in any case other reasons for some modification of the old undoctrinal habits of mind and action. The rise of large industrial monopolies and the simultaneous enlargement of the industrial unions had made relations in industry more impersonal, more a matter of the abstractions of capital and labour. This way of looking at things was fostered by the evident tenderness of anti-labour governments to private enterprise during the 'twenties and 'thirties, as in their sale to private capitalists on cheap terms of a number of state industrial enterprises which had been established by labour, and which, despite a normal share of failures, had for the most part a good record of public service and profitable running. The part played by the banks in blocking the policies of labour governments during the depression still further strengthened the sense of irreconcilable conflict; and as depression lifted, the world's drift into totalitarianism and war deepened political divisions in Australia as elsewhere.

There is no reason, however, to believe that former habits of mind have been radically changed. Cynicism towards the protestations of wealth has been traditional in Australian radicalism, and a readiness to suspect the political influence of large companies and of politicians sympathetic to them is no new thing. A scrutiny of Australian affairs during the last thirty years leaves the impression that an uncompromising theoretical temper has been throughout less typical than a compromising bargaining temper. In fact, Australian political life has been less marked by attachment to theory than by a habit of making concessions to organized sectional interests, with this check that the small percentage of swinging voters who determine the fate of Australian political parties demands in general that concessions shall not all go one way.

But the depression made clear a major and persistent division between the political parties. It found in office the first federal labour government since 1917. That government was unable to carry out the plan of its able treasurer, E. G. Theodore, a plan which then seemed boldly inflationary but resembled more than any of the rival plans then in the field the policies now generally favoured. It was unable to do so, not only because the government was opposed by a hostile majority in the Senate or Upper House, but because it had no full control over certain bodies outside parliament which could in large part shape the monetary and borrowing policy of the country.

Public borrowing had since 1927 been placed in the hands of the Loan Council which consisted of representatives of the Commonwealth and State governments but was responsible to no one government. More important in the depression was the independence of the Commonwealth Bank and the trading banks. The question was raised which has not ceased to divide Australian politics: whether in the last resort the making of economic policy was to be completely in the hands of the government responsible to parliament, or in part in the hands of bodies reserved from government interference.

In 1924 the Nationalist-Country Party Government had reconstituted the Commonwealth Bank. It had given it the functions of a central bank; it had placed it under an independent governing board consisting for the most part of men with experience in large-scale financial, commercial and industrial undertakings; and it had withdrawn the note issue from political control.

It is clear that in the depression this board rather than the governments determined the limitations within which recovery plans could be devised. The stringent retrenchment of wages, salaries and government expenditure, laid down by the Commonwealth Bank Board in February 1931 as the condition on which it would assist the governments, ran clean counter to Theodore's proposals. He sought to overcome the bank's opposition to his policy by a Fiduciary Notes Bill and a Commonwealth Bank Amendment Bill. Both were defeated in the Senate. In April, the bank declared a limit to its short-term lending to the governments, and in effect forced the premiers, assisted by a number of economists, to adopt 'the Premiers' Plan'.

This plan accepted the retrenchments, and, in return for an undertaking to balance their budgets, the governments gained a limited amount of credit through the Commonwealth Bank. The pound had already been devalued on the initiative of the Bank of New South Wales and was pegged at 25 per cent below sterling in order to assist export prices. Despite some conservative cries of theft, wage and salary cuts were paralleled by a reduction, by means of conversion, of interest rates on overseas as well as internal loans. The Premiers' Plan, in short, balanced its deflationary elements with mild inflation. It was, within the limited range of possibilities open to its devisers, a genuine attempt at compromise, a genuine attempt to spread sacrifice over the community as a whole.

Meanwhile, labour supporters of different policies were routed.
E. G. Theodore's proposals were too novel to gain the complete
adherence of his own party. Two groups split away from the government, one attaching itself to the policies of the radical but quite
undoctrinal premier of New South Wales, J. T. Lang, the other
fusing with the nationalists to form the United Australia Party. The
elections of 1931 returned a federal government of this latter fusion,
led by J. A. Lyons, who had been member of the preceding Labour
Government.

These experiences left an enduring impression on the Labour
Party and Labour's policy of full employment after the Second
World War, together with its corollary of control of banking policy,
were the products of those years. The rightness or wrongness of the
conflicting policies of the depression years is a matter of less lasting
importance than labour's discovery in emergency that, as the government of the commonwealth, it could not control one of the major
policy-making bodies in the country's political economy. That
discovery was not to be forgotten.

At the cost of great wretchedness, the depression brought greater
health into the Australian economy. Inefficient industries went under
and others learnt an increase in efficiency. The fall in overseas credits
made it necessary to buy less from outside and to make more at
home, and the long-run effect was to stimulate renewed industrial
expansion, aided by lower costs. Despite the depression, the industrial
expansion of the 'thirties was both more varied and faster than that
of the 'twenties. In 1936 the Tariff Board reported,

The growth of Australian secondary industries is marked by an increase
in the variety of goods manufactured under reasonable rates of duty
rather than by an increase in the general level of protective duties. Many
industries are now able to sell their products at prices little, if any, above
the costs of duty-free importations from the United Kingdom; the
prices of some locally made goods are even below the costs of duty-free
imports.

It was a mark of Australia's industrialization that the share
of manufactures in the total value of production rose between
1928–9 and 1938–9 from 36 to 42 per cent while the share of the
pastoral industry declined from 26 to less than 20 per cent. In
this development, the iron and steel industries played the major
role.

As Australia was recovering from the depression and seeking
greater stability in foreign trade, so greatly disturbed by the economic

nationalism of the 'thirties in which she had fully shared, world war came as a third hammer-blow in this century to any assumption of sheltered security. The great changes wrought in Australia by the years of war had their roots in developments before it; the war quickened the pace of change and made its nature evident.

I I

AUSTRALIA; PRESENT AND FUTURE

The changes which have taken place in Australia since war broke out in 1939 have indeed been so great and are still, thirty years later, continuing at such a pace, that it is both easy to forget their pre-war beginnings, and difficult to isolate the permanent from the ephemeral elements in our situation.

Throughout its colonial history, Australia had been sheltered by the unrivalled power of the British fleet. There had been invasion scares but no danger of permanent conquest. But the fall of Singapore to the Japanese only confirmed a change in the balance of power which had already taken place. The time had long passed when British naval power in eastern waters could match the Japanese, while Pearl Harbour delayed the deployment of American power which could do so. The withdrawal of Britain 'East of Suez' in our own day is only the completion of an unavoidable process.

Australia could no longer shelter behind Britain. The fall of Singapore, the dropping of Japanese bombs on Australian soil, and the penetration of Japanese troops to within thirty-two miles of Port Moresby, separated from the Australian mainland only by Torres Strait, jolted Australians into a perception of their insecurity which the uneasy aftermath of the war did nothing to dull.

Australia's security is endangered from outside by the domestic uncertainties of the new nations to its north, from Indonesia through the Malayan Peninsula to Burma and Indo-China. It is menaced by the precarious state of power relations in south-eastern Asia, particularly since the victory in China of a Communist Party still committed to a belief in world revolution. And it could be endangered by the contrast between a country of small population, high living standards and attractive mineral resources and the Asian countries of large populations and low living standards.

Insurgent nationalism in the countries north of Australia put it out of the question to base security in this area simply on agreement between its European ruling powers. Asian nationalism was not a product of the war, but war gave it victory. The precise shape of these new nations and of their governments might remain in doubt, but not their independence. This was a fact of our situation which we had to accept, and indeed Australian policy towards new-born Indonesia quickly illustrated a disposition to accept the fact of Asian nationalism and to seek some enduring relationship with its more stable elements. And if this policy was established by the Labour Party, it has been amply confirmed by its opponents, the Liberal–Country Party Coalition, in their turn.

But what precisely should that relationship be? The Australian answer to the precarious state of international relations has always been experimental rather than doctrinal. The progressive withdrawal of Great Britain from Singapore and Malaysia, for example, has posed the question how far Australia should step into Great Britain's shoes. The answer given in 1969, not to the entire satisfaction of Malaysia, is a readiness to assist in the defence of the region but an unreadiness to shoulder the burden which Britain has put down. And this must be the answer. Australia, though affluent, has neither the numbers nor the resources to become the policeman of the area. It can play a role of some importance in association with greater powers, but this role must for a long time to come be that of a secondary power which may hope, if its counsels are wise, to influence but not to make policy.

The first independent Australian diplomatic missions were established in 1940 when ministers were accredited to the United States and Japan, and these two powers and their policies, particularly in relation to China, must be the major determinants of Australian foreign policy for many years to come. The dual nature of this dependence has been obscured, since the fall of Singapore, by our single-minded movement into an American orbit; but politics have a habit of following economics and economics suggest a growing dependence on Japan, our best customer without whose insatiable thirst for Australian coal and metals our present rate of economic growth would be much less. The 1957 trade treaty with Japan not only put aside as irrelevant the aftermath of wartime hostility but showed a realistic assessment of coming opportunities, if only the one-sided restrictiveness, so disastrously displayed in the 1936 'trade diversion policy' and so dear to manufacturers in search of protection at home and markets abroad, were avoided. In 1966–7, 21·1 per cent of Australia's exports went to Japan compared with 14 per cent to the

F

United Kingdom and 13·2 per cent to the United States, and the Japanese share of foreign investment in Australian enterprises, though still minute when compared with the British and American share, is nevertheless growing.

Australian policy-makers in the future, therefore, may be found to be giving increasing attention to Japanese views; and this, paradoxically enough, could in the course of time, by offering practicable alternatives, lend some degree of independence to Australian decisions. But the movement of policy since the disasters of 1941–2 has been strongly towards an almost complete reliance on the United States. The ANZUS Treaty of 1951, although vague about precise commitments, made it clear that the United States would regard the safety of Australia and New Zealand as vital to its own security. In 1954 an attempt was made to link the ANZUS countries with the United Kingdom and some Asian countries in a defensive alliance against communist aggression in South-East Asia; but SEATO, the South East Asia Treaty Organization, has remained of marginal value because of the abstention of such Asian nations as Japan which saw in it a threat of involvement in policies not of their own making.

Australian acceptance of American leadership has extended to the despatch of Australian forces to Vietnam. Up to this point there had been little disposition to question the readiness of Australian governments to follow the American lead; nor were Australians in general troubled by any contrast between their traditional ties with Britain and their actual dependence on the United States. But Vietnam raised very acutely the question whether Australian dependence on American power must entail a complete surrender of initiative. For Australians, like Americans, have been deeply divided about Vietnam. It is clear, at least, that Australian governments have yet to discover how to unite an acceptance of the fundamentals of American policies with independent and constructive criticism. But practice may be more independent than talk, and Australian governments happily arrange sales of wheat to a mainland Chinese government which they do not diplomatically recognize. And their participation in the regular meetings of ASPAC, the Asian and Pacific Council, exposes their views and policies to the influence of frank discussion between the foreign ministers of a wide range of governments.

In the meantime more constructive foundations of security are being laid in programmes of aid to under-developed countries. As part of the Colombo Plan Australia had, to June 1966, contributed $129,038,000, partly for projects of economic development and partly for technical assistance and scholarships. To the end of 1966, over 6,900 training awards had been made under the plan. A further amount of $89,308,000 had been contributed up to June 1966, through the United Nations 'specialized agencies' such as the United Nations Children's Fund and the World Food Programme, while $47,000,000 had been contributed to the World Bank and close on $80,000,000 promised to the new Asia Development Bank to assist development in Asia. A similar concern to promote economic development as a recognized prerequisite of stability is shown by official Australian participation in the Asian Development Bank and in ECAFE, the Economic Commission for Asia and the Far East.

But even when the considerable sums of private aid through such organizations as Community Aid abroad, Red Cross and the World Student Service are added, it is arguable that Australia could, reasonably and indeed in its own interest, do more when the accumulated totals of aid abroad are set against an annual defence expenditure which reached $1,115,000,000 in 1967–8. In our struggle for security, armament is a poor second to the building of economic stability to our north.

Nearer home, Australia has a more direct responsibility to build a new and workable nation in its Territory of Papua–New Guinea. This territory is both incomplete, in that similar peoples of the main island are cut off from it by the incorporation of West Irian in Indonesia, and too inclusive, in that it includes some islands, such as Bougainville, many of whose people look to the Solomon Islands rather than to Port Moresby. In any case, it draws no cohesion from its own history; for its many separate peoples, speaking many different languages, range from stone age tribesmen to Europeanized town-dwellers. Unity and cohesion will come to it, if at all, from the Australian Administration, and only if those policies of the Administration which encourage a sense of common nationhood overcome those actions which arouse local resentments.

The task has not been made easier by some past sins of omission and commission. History divided the Territory into two administrations—Papua, transferred to Australia by Great Britain in 1902, and the former German New Guinea, captured by an Australian force in 1914, kept under military rule for six years, and then separately administered as an Australian mandate. Sir Hubert Murray's wise rule of Papua protected its 200,000 Papuans from too rapid disintegration of their tribal life; but the positive aspect of his policy of controlled development was slowed down both by the relative poverty of Papua which lacked New Guinea's gold-mines and population, and by the limitation of the Australian Commonwealth Government's expenditure to £45,000 a year.

New Guinea's larger local revenue, £500,000 in 1939 compared with Papua's £190,000, enabled its Adminstration to set up more hospitals and more primary schools than Papua; but in both territorories, there was a failure to develop secondary education, the necessary base for any venture into tertiary education and self-government. Agricultural development was handicapped by too great a concentration on copra and rubber, the prices of which slumped badly in the inter-war period. And low revenues made it impossible to attract enough first-class Australians to the two territorial services, although some outstanding men were attracted to them, but not by money.

Nevertheless, the native peoples were protected from the worst accompaniments of white settlement. Before the Second World War, there was no sense of urgency and, indeed, some belief on leaving the people alone, beyond a minimum of pacification. The post-war world is different. It has seen the rapid dissolution of colonial empires, and, as the administrator of a United Nations Trust Territory, the former Mandate, Australia has been exposed to a great deal of international pressure, some of it hypocritical, some of it ignorant, to hurry the granting of independence. There is no question that the Territory must be prepared for self-government, and with a much greater sense of urgency. But much has to be done to train peoples who have been only a few years ago primitive tribesmen for peaceful survival and development in a difficult world.

Australia's post-war record in the Territory has been on the whole good, although there are some danger signals to be noted. The Native Local Government Councils set up under the Papua and New Guinea Act of 1949 have trained increasing numbers of people in local self-government, over 900,000 or more than half the population by 1964. The Legislative Council established in 1951 was progressively liberalised to give indigenous members a greater share in central policy-making, and in 1963 the Legislative Council was replaced by a House of Assembly of sixty-four members, ten appointed, ten elected by special electorates of non-indigenous voters, and forty-four elected in open electorates. The first election gave a majority to indigenous members. The allowance of $1,900 per annum allows native members to give their time to politics. With all its difficulties of language and inexperience the House of Assembly has worked well and responsibly as a training centre, although final power still rests with the Administrator, who may veto its ordinances, and with the Australian Government which instructs the Administrator and provides two-thirds of the public revenue. There has been proper restraint in the use of these powers of tutelage.

But responsible self-government must rest finally on a foundation of education ripened by experience. The House of Assembly may nurture in its members a sense of nationhood, except in those islanders who resent incorporation in the Territory; but only spreading education can instil this sense into the electors. The Currie Commission of 1963 on higher education in the Territory stressed the importance of post-primary education and recommended the establishment of an Institute of Higher Technical Education and of a University. These institutions are at work and have attracted to them some men of outstanding probity and intelligence. If the decisive role of university trained Maoris in the revival of the Maori people in New Zealand may serve as a guide, one may predict that these men and their students will make or mar the new political community of New Guinea.

The Australian Government has taken good advice in building up post primary education; it is not clear that this wise initiative is being adequately supported with money. That is one of the danger signs referred to, for there are always old hands willing to advise treasury-haunted officials to go slow with the dangerous business of education.

There are other danger signals. Differential rates of pay in the territorial service may be more costly in building resentment than equal rates would be in money. And recent native opposition in Bougainville to the resumption of native lands in order to allow mining development points to another problem of great difficulty. There is no doubt that such ventures will bring material prosperity to the Territory; but clearly they need much patient exposition to the local peoples, and much care and generosity in determining and explaining compensation. To quote Australian land and mining laws to people who do not understand them is disingenuous and to rest on a vote of the House of Assembly may be merely provocative to people who do not happily accept their attachment to the main island of New Guinea. The example merely illustrates the delicacy and difficulty of a time of transition from tribalism to the twentieth century. Australian good-will is not lacking and Australian Administration in the Territory has many achievements to its credit. Its more difficult task lies ahead of it, that of leading people of diverse languages, loyalties and stages of culture to a capacity for stable and progressive self-government.

But Australians have a responsibility for native peoples much nearer home. After many generations of putting the fate of the Australian aborigines out of sight and out of mind, Australians have in recent years become aware, and, to an increasing degree, sympathetically aware of the difficulties under which aborigines labour, although one may doubt whether many beyond a few anthropologists[1] can fully understand the personal conflict of the aborigine who breaks his spears and walks into the town where perhaps his children may gain at school from his renunciation. Policies of assimilation speeded up the process and there are now few aborigines living in an untouched tribal state.

Assimilation is being challenged by more subtle policies of integration which hope to preserve the aborigine's memory of tribal tradition and pride in it while bringing him as an equal member into the larger community. But it is easier to preach integration than to make it work, and easier to make it work with tribal aborigines than with the fringe-dwellers of the towns. Fringe-dwellers who have lost the guidance of tribal lore and loyalties while still spiritually as well as geographically outside the white community are rootless people. Certain things can be done to give them consolation and hope, by improving their housing, reducing infant mortality, and teaching their children—and the teaching must contain respect for their past as well as understanding of their future needs. It will require on the part of the white Australians a patience and sensitivity rarely found, to carry the policy of integration through without ugly developments of race-prejudice, which, nevertheless, has diminished.

The fringe-dweller, still more common in country towns than in the great cities, is one aspect of the aboriginal problem and a growing aspect. The distorting of a planned aboriginal policy by concession to economic interests is another. It was difficult enough to get an aboriginal policy at all when aboriginal affairs were matters for the States, outside the Northern Territory which is administered by the Commonwealth. Conferences of Commonwealth and State Ministers concerned with aboriginal welfare, and more recently, the establishment of a Commonwealth Department of Aboriginal Affairs under a Minister passionately concerned for aboriginal welfare, have generated positive policies to unite protection with integration.

One question is what priority these policies are to be allowed among the other purposes of government. Commonwealth support to an international consortium's development of bauxite in Arnhem Land, an aboriginal reserve, has put this question sharply. It is not possible to delay the development of important national resources indefinitely, nor can they be developed by the aborigines. And some of the advocates of aboriginal rights, who have indeed done much to stir the public conscience, may, by pressing unrealistic demands too far, bring failure to constructive policies of welfare.

On the other hand, the Commonwealth Government cannot be

[1] W. E. H. Stanner, *After the Dreaming* (Boyer lectures, A.B.C.), 1968.

cleared of too quick a readiness to forget its aboriginal policies, perhaps not unanimously supported in the Government itself, when mining interests conflict with them. White Australians have a duty to demand that aboriginal interests be given serious consideration, and that aboriginal assets should receive proper and negotiated compensation in all such cases. It is equally important that all aboriginal sacred places should be respected. For perhaps few peoples have had such an intimate and profound relation with their land as the aborigines for whom it is peopled with their ancestral lore.

Australians have generally prided themselves on their tolerance, although the cynic might remark that tolerance was easy when the problem was not under your nose in Sydney or Melbourne but a thousand miles away in Katharine or Darwin. The recent history of the white Australian's dealings with the aborigines suggests some growth in tested tolerance. So does the recent history of Australian immigration policies.

The restrictive immigration policies of the late nineteenth-century colonies and the early Commonwealth were established when all that most Australians knew of the Far East was what they saw or imagined of poverty-stricken Cantonese coolies whom some saw as the first trickle of a deluge and some, including many of the same, saw as a cheap and competing labour supply. The latter fear was actively spread by *Bulletin* cartoonists who depicted Chinese coolies as the instruments by which Mr Fatman enslaved the workers. That situation has been radically changed, to the point that Gallup Polls suggest a majority in favour of a quota for Asian immigrants.

Full employment has much to do with this change as it has with the universal acceptance of a high rate of European immigration. So has improved knowledge and wider experience. The Asians whom the Australian at home meets today are the officials, the merchants or the students, and, very importantly, their wives; while by way of travel, business, diplomacy and study, his knowledge of Asia is being rapidly increased. The growth of Indian, Indonesian and Oriental Studies in the Universities is giving a deeper thrust to such knowledge, while the teaching of Asian languages has gained at least a toe-hold in the secondary schools, to provide the keys to that deeper knowledge.

In keeping with this change, both the law and the administration of immigration restrictions have been liberalized. The dictation test adopted in 1901 has been abolished; in practice it had long given way to an understanding with Asian Governments by which they limited the issue of passports valid for Australia to merchants and students. And if Asian immigration is not actively encouraged,

Asians with skills recognized by the Immigration Department to be wanted in Australia may gain permission to stay permanently.

For many Australians, this seems too little and they argue for a quota. The official reply is that a quota would prove restrictive and this may be correct; for some time to come more may be achieved by liberalizing administrative practice than by challenging old fears.

The continuing change of attitudes towards Asian immigration has been accompanied by, and may indeed be part of, a change of attitude towards immigration in general. High levels of unemployment in the 1920s at the time of post-war immigration schemes provoked strong hostility to immigration, particularly in the unions. Humanity overcame this to some degree before the Second World War when some thousands of refugees from Nazism were assisted to come to Australia. Similar grounds of humanity existed after the war in the millions of displaced persons in Europe. But the Labour Government which broke from its traditions and launched the great post-war immigration scheme in 1945 did so for other motives as well, for immigration was seen partly as a defence measure, but still more as part of a programme of development.

So indeed it has proved, despite the short-run inflationary effects of a high rate of immigration in the time of post-war shortages, to the solution of which the skills and labour of the immigrants themselves contributed. Since 1945 over 2,000,000 immigrants have come to Australia.

Not only has this immigration been an important part of the increase which carried the population from 7,000,000 at the end of the war to 12,000,000 in 1968 and may be expected to carry it to 20,000,000 at the end of the century; it has also changed the composition of the Australian people. Like the gold-rush immigration, the early post-war immigration of displaced persons brought with it a high proportion of skilled persons, some with skills new to the country. It also varied the national derivations of the Australian population to a noticeable degree, somewhat over half the immigrants coming from non-British countries. In the early post-war years, the largest number of non-British immigrants were displaced persons from the Baltic countries; but in later years, in addition to a steady flow from Scandinavia, Germany, Holland and Greece, the largest non-British section has been Italian, Italy having supplied some half-million migrants.

Such an immigration could not be introduced without some strain and it required a painful education for both Australians and 'New Australians'. Nevertheless, the immigrants have been absorbed remarkably well, particularly since an unimaginative policy of 'assimilation' gave way to one of 'integration' which recognized that to encourage in the immigrants some pride in their own cultural tradition might not only lubricate the process of adaptation to a new country, but even contribute to that country's cultural variety.

The demographic and economic results of the immigration are tangible, in numbers, and in a more adequate home market and industrial base for exports. Some of its cultural results are also visible, as in improved eating facilities; but the most important cultural results may exist in the stimulus of new traditions to artistic and intellectual life.

A high rate of immigration is an agreed policy of all parties and is accepted as basic to Australian development. It could be adopted in the first place because it was viewed in the context of new policies of social welfare and of full employment; it could be continued because the sustained rate of development, apart from a minor recession in 1961–2, has kept the demand for labour high. Australia's Gross National Product measured at constant prices has maintained an average annual rate of increase of 4·3 per cent since 1950, although there have been some considerable fluctuations of the rate within this period.

But when the Labour Government adopted the policy of assisted immigration in 1945, these results were in the future and, in view of Labour's earlier suspicion of immigration, its adoption can be understood only by relating it to the simultaneous guarantees to the unions contained in the policies of 'national welfare' and 'full employment'.

In 1939 Australians, despite their reputation for leaning on government, were spending less per head on social services than the people of Great Britain. All parties agreed that the functions of the State in this respect had to be enlarged, though they differed considerably in detail, the non-labour parties preferring contributory schemes, the Labour Party preferring to finance social services from taxation as a means of re-distributing incomes.

Various proposals for comprehensive schemes of national insurance made from the eve of the first world war to the eve of the second world war had petered out in disputes between those who feared high taxation and those who opposed contributory schemes. Nevertheless, the Depression made the necessity of some national scheme painfully evident, while the Second World War, although it caused the indefinite postponement of a truncated act at last passed in 1938, established the high rate of taxation which national welfare would require. And both depression and war nurtured a determination that peace should usher in a better Australia. If this aspiration had adherents in all parties, it was a matter of personal faith with the Labour Prime Ministers, Mr Curtin and Mr Chifley.

For the Labour Party, social services, which were grouped together under its 'National Welfare Scheme', were the complement of its major policy of social security, 'full employment'. In October 1942 a joint parliamentary committee had pointed out that the problem of social insecurity was not only to provide for its victims but to reduce its causes; and it had urged expert investigation and planning to this end. The Government's response was the creation of the Minstry of Post-War Reconstruction, and the announcement by the Federal Treasurer, Mr J. B. Chifley, in a financial statement in February 1943, of the twin policies of 'national welfare' and of maintaining a high level of employment.

Indeed, a sentiment for social justice, which had been vague as to means, was at this time crystallized into a comprehensive policy, under pressure of war and the necessity to plan post-war reconstruction. It is the active pursuit of this policy that makes the period of labour rule from 1941–9 stand out, whether its results are viewed with favour or dislike, as one of the decisive epochs in the shaping of the Australian community.

The 1940s saw many of the blank spaces on the chart of social services filled in. In view of the dubious legality of Commonwealth intervention in a sphere of state sovereignty, a referendum was held in 1946 which gave the Commonwealth wide power to legislate for social services. A measure, before inflation greatly upset its accuracy, of this enlargement of Commonwealth government is the increase of expenditure on social services from £16,000,000 in 1938–9 to £88,000,000 in 1947–8 and to £123,000,000 in 1949–50. Nevertheless, it proved extremely difficult to get agreement to a scheme of medical benefits. Opposition of the British Medical Association in Australia to the Government's scheme of medical benefits cut down this aspect of national welfare to the provision of a range of free or nearly free medicines and to a contribution to hospital bills, until the Liberal Government of Mr R. G. Menzies tried a different approach in the early 1950s. By this scheme, the Commonwealth contributed towards the payment of hospital and medical fees for those people who themselves contributed to an approved hospital benefits association. This scheme has operated for close on twenty years but remains a subject of controversy, and the Commonwealth Government has now before it a report by a Committee under the chairmanship of Mr Justice Nimmo on its defects and possible improvement.

The policy of full employment, proposed by the wartime Labour Government as the other component of its 'National Welfare Scheme' had its roots in the Depression, memory of which had not ceased to govern labour policy. Wartime experience of the possible uses of economic controls helped to bridge the gap between aims and detailed policy. The policy was set out in a White Paper of May 1945. While its main thesis resembled that of Beveridge's *Full Employment in a Free Society*, and while it was to be seen in the context of similar discussions in Canada and the United States as well as in Great Britain, its local roots were evident in its opening paragraphs:

Despite the need for more houses, food, equipment and every other type of product, before the war not all those available for work were able to find employment or to feel a sense of security in their future. On the average during the twenty years between 1919 and 1939 more than one-tenth of the men and women desiring work were unemployed. In the worst period of the depression well over 25 per cent were left in unproductive idleness. By contrast, during the war no financial or other obstacles have been allowed to prevent the need for extra production being satisfied to the limit of our resources. It is true that wartime full employment has been accompanied by efforts and sacrifices and a curtailment of individual liberties which only the supreme emergency of war could justify; but it has shown up the wastes of unemployment in pre-war years, and it has taught us valuable lessons which we can apply to the problems of peace-time, when full employment must be achieved in ways consistent with a free society.

No post-war government would fully oppose the policy outlined in the White Paper, that is, to balance the falling away of private spending by an increase of government expenditure on capital equipment; but it was evident, nevertheless, that the policy of full employment would have a stormy passage. For it could require the imposition of a public plan of development on an economy that was not fully open to public control in time of peace, both because of its large measure of private enterprise and because of the constitutional limits set on the powers of the Commonwealth Government.

These problems became the subject of bitter political controversy when the Government proposed, as a means to its full employment policy, to ensure the right of government to control banking policy. In a passage that harked back to the controversies of the depression years between the Commonwealth Bank Board and the Labour Government of that time, the White Paper warned 'that it will be the responsibility of the Commonwealth Bank to ensure that the banking system does not initiate a general contraction of credit or contribute in any way to the growth of unemployment through a decline of expenditure'.

In 1945 the Government amended the Commonwealth Bank Act
to ensure, among other things, that in the last resort the financial
policy of the Commonwealth Bank—and, indirectly, of the trading
banks—could be brought into harmony with the policy of the government of the day. When some aspects of that legislation were declared
unconstitutional by the High Court, the Government passed a Bill
in 1947 to nationalize the trading banks. This Bill became the
subject of a political and judicial battle which ended in the defeat of
the Labour Government in the election of 1949 and in the rejection
as unconstitutional of a large part of its Banking Act, both by the
High Court of Australia and by the Judicial Committee of the Privy
Council.

In the course of heated controversy, labour policy was often
denounced as doctrinaire socialism. It is true that the proposal to
nationalize the banks, which for many labour men was an after-
thought based on the fear that the more temperate Bill of 1945 would
be legally challenged in crisis, went beyond majority opinion. On
the whole, however, the full-employment policy of the Labour
Government may prove in the perspective of time to be a typical
experimental compromise. If it insists on controlling private enterprise for the sake of social security, it refuses to accept the assumption
of a war of labour and capital in which there can be no quarter given
and no enduring treaty made.

Nor is the mixture of government and private enterprise new,
though the ingredients have from time to time been mixed in varying
proportions. Early in our history, drought and distance imposed on
governments the task of providing such utilities as railways and
irrigation; and their number and extent has grown. It has been
accepted without question that it is the proper duty of governments
to provide such services.

Labour has from time to time gone farther and established state
enterprises competing with private enterprise, partly to break price-
rings, and combines, partly to supply government needs. Non-labour
governments have from time to time wound up such enterprises and
sold them to private concerns. The pendulum swings, but the field of
government continues to enlarge through the alternations of expansion and contraction; for the needs of defence and national development push all governments, irrespective of theory, into enlargement
of government enterprise.

The mixture of a measure of public control of the economy with
private enterprise is likewise traditional. Here also, while the proportions fluctuate, the trend is on the whole towards increase of state
control. The exigencies of two wars and the depression, added to

the public demand that economic activities shall conform to certain standards of social justice, have hastened this development.

The report of the Committee of Economic Enquiry, 1965—the 'Vernon Report'—offered wise advice on this subject, arguing for a sophisticated assessment of economic aims and achievements without dictation, by means of an advisory body on the lines of the Economic Council of Canada which could review and report on the economy, act as a forum of consultation and communication, and promote and publish research. 'The paramount need, as we see it', the Committee reported, 'is for governments, industry and the public to have access to the best assessment of what is economically possible and of the dangers that must be avoided or overcome if the economy is to achieve its maximum of potential for growth with stability. This would provide the proper atmosphere for concerted action to convert the objectives of economic policy into reality.'

The high rate and changing components of development make continuous reassessment necessary. For the Second World War forced a rapid unfolding of a new phase in Australia's industrial growth. This phase had begun earlier, but the needs of war speeded its pace, when Australia was compelled to make unthought-of demands of its electrical, chemical and metallurgical industries. Post-war discoveries of metals, oil and natural gas on a scale inconceivable to pre-war geology have been justly described as themselves producing a revolution in the Australian economy, and have been the major attraction for the inflow of foreign capital at a rate which has contributed strongly to the exuberant and buoyant tone of the economy for most of the post-war years.

The results are evident in swelling cities, rapidly changing skylines, lavish spending and a tendency of imports, from time to time, to outrun overseas reserves. It is accepted governmental policy to maintain a high rate of immigration and development, while defending overseas reserves. The dependence of this policy on continued overseas investment in Australia is evident, reduced only by the degree to which the value of Australian exports can be increased.

It is to increase of exports that Australia must look to protect its economy from those dangers which accompany the undoubted advantages of a high rate of capital inflow. There has been much public discussion of the respective advantages and dangers of our present degree of dependence on overseas capital, ranging too extremely from the fear that we may lose control of our natural resources over to arguments that only foreign capital can develop them. More soberly, the Vernon Committee 'heavily discounted . . . narrowly nationalistic objections to overseas investment', while nevertheless observing the dangers of relying too much on capital inflow for balance of payments. The committee further noticed that Australians could properly seek more information on the attitude of foreign companies to such matters as an increasing Australian share in ownership, export franchises, the development in Australia of special skills, take-overs and the use of locally-raised funds. It is clear that Australian governments of whatever party must impose on the exploitation of mineral resources by foreign companies conditions which protect national interests ranging from aboriginal welfare to maintaining stability in development. But the essential protection of Australian interests against the risks of a large capital inflow must be an aggressive export policy to improve the balance of trade, and encouragement of domestic saving.

At no period of its history since the gold-rushes over a century ago has Australia experienced changes so varied and so marked as those of the present generation. For some years after the Second World War, development was dammed back by the inescapable difficulties of the transition from war to peace. Scarcity of labour, increased by the necessity of retraining ex-servicemen and of training these and others for entirely new processes, was only one of many shortages. The most important material shortage was that of power; for Australia's suddenly increased needs of power for both industrial and domestic use required large capital works which could not quickly be completed and the importing of equipment for which the world-wide demand outran supply. During these years, too many projects competed for the available resources of capital, labour and materials; and it was not always easy to decide between domestic housing, so far behind the need, and industrial works, or possible to avoid imposing controls as the only alternative to chaos. With immigration adding its own to these other inflationary pressures, it is not difficult to understand the mood of considerable restiveness which marked the late 1940s and the early 1950s.

Shortages were worsened by an increase of industrial stoppages. They were probably worsened also by the demand for a shorter working week which was met by the Commonwealth Arbitration Court's award of a forty-hour week and which for some time seems not to have been fully balanced by increased output. If this failure stood at the doors of management as well as of workers, delays and shortages encouraged many people to see in industrial disputes the main or only cause of their troubles and to rest their cure on the cry for disciplinary measures.

For the unionists, the benefits of full employment, shorter hours and rising wages were diminished by rapidly rising prices. Irritation joined with the tactical advantage of the shortage of labour to encourage an increase of strikes and a readiness in certain unions to follow the leadership of communist and left-wing leaders. It is probable that this was support to those who promised action rather than to their doctrines; and when the Chifley Labour Government took strong action against an unjustified coal strike in 1949, all the efforts of communist leaders to organize stoppages and protests on a wide scale failed. Indeed, it seemed that unionists were themselves tired of the recurrent interruptions to work and pay, and despite numerous skirmishes in public transport and on the waterfront, there followed a period of relative tranquillity in industrial relations.

This result was not immediately evident to all. Communist leadership had lost a battle in 1949; had it abandoned the war? The Liberal Government of Mr R. G. Menzies which took office in 1949 did not think so and proposed to do something about it. Australia had not, and as a highly industrialized society could not, escape the world's unrest and its ideological divisions. There are undemocratic minorities at both extremes of the political spectrum, and many people of undemocratic sentiment who belong to neither; but the vast majority of Australians are neither tempted nor persuaded by totalitarian or revolutionary ideologies. They have fought their domestic battles militantly but within the framework of their common acceptance of parliamentary democracy. A creed which regards that acceptance as a delusion blinding the working class to the necessity of the revolutionary class-struggle runs clean counter to Australian political habits, and is equally opposed by the labour and non-labour parties.

The Labour Party resisted the pressure put upon it to outlaw the Communist Party, relying on such existing laws as the Crimes Act to deal with acts of sedition or treason, and on its social security policy to defeat communism by satisfying the needs and removing the tensions in which it bred. No party would entirely deny the thesis that an active policy of social reform would at least weaken the influence of those who seek a radical subversion of society. But the Liberal and Country Parties took the view that the major cause of lagging production and industrial strife in the post-war years was a communist conspiracy so serious, particularly in the context of uncertain international relations, that it must be suppressed, even at the expense of a departure from traditional liberties.

In accordance with this view, the Liberal and Country Party Government led by Mr R. G. Menzies brought in a Bill to outlaw the Communist Party and to prevent 'declared' communists from holding office in the commonwealth public service and trade unions. This

Bill deeply divided the community, because to some degree it sought to outlaw an opinion and because in large measure it threw on the accused person the onus of proving that he was not a communist according to the wide definition contained in the Bill. It was also argued that the mere accusation, even if successfully rebutted, would, in the existing state of feeling, seriously damage the accused person's security and prospects. On such grounds, the Labour Party used its majority in the Senate to delay the Bill for many months, but at length gave way to a section in its own ranks and allowed the Bill to pass. In March 1951 it was declared invalid by the High Court of Australia, while in October a referendum seeking power to enact such legislation was narrowly defeated. A more hopeful approach to the problem was contained in amendments of 1949 and 1951 to the Commonwealth Conciliation and Arbitration Act which were designed to prevent communist 'rigging' of trade-union elections. The first, made by the Government of Mr Chifley, allowed an industrial organization, or branch of it, to ask the Industrial Registrar to conduct an election on its behalf. The second, made by the Government of Mr Menzies, both allowed a prescribed number of members of the organization to request the Industrial Registrar to conduct the election, and tightened up the rules governing union elections.

The 1950s and 1960s were decades of such dramatic material progress and prosperity as to push these problems to the background. They were not thereby removed. On the face of it, the Communist Party lost ground in this period. It lost ground in union elections, while such external events as Kruschev's denunciation of Stalin and the Russian suppression of the Hungarian revolt in 1956 lost it both members and sympathizers. This was not necessarily a weakening in its own determination, and the determined remnant may be more dangerous to an easy-going democracy than the more diluted party of earlier years. On the other hand, Australian democracy, like any other, can also be endangered by those who denounce every independent and unpopular opinion as 'communist', thereby encouraging in liberal-minded people habits of timidity and hypocrisy which amount to public irresponsibility. Australia escaped McCarthyism, but there was a period when it ran close to catching that contagion. Perhaps the worst threat of the Communist Party to the democracy in peacetime is that it could stir a renewal of that fever.

It has been the argument of this book, however, that Australian political life has developed a strong and resilient tradition of practical but experimental compromise. This sprang in the first place from our British inheritance of parliamentary democracy. It took on its local variations as a result of the stimulus given to aspirations of social equality by the social unsettlement of migration and the struggle for livelihood in a difficult environment.

With all its faults, this was a militant, idealistic tradition, tempered in the end by a readiness to come to practical compromises, if only after the heat and dust of conflict. Fundamentally, it consisted in a readiness to experiment by adaptation to circumstances rather than by the wholesale imposition of doctrinaire systems. At its worst it could degenerate into a mere competition between sectional interests; at its best it could show flexible adaptation to circumstance. At times, the flame of genuine idealism has burnt brightly, even among politicians; at others, it has almost flickered out, and the decline of faith has expressed itself in too widespread a disposition of wise men and true to turn their backs on politics as a dirty business.

There is a fashion among some Australian commentators at this time to engage in jeremiads about the state of the Commonwealth, finding timidity replacing courage, conformity innovation, and imitation originality in an 'Austerica' which no longer dares to be itself. It is of course a serious question whether the Australian tradition of militant but practical idealism can survive in a country now fully exposed to those forces in the world which, by reason either of their complexities or of their dangers, breed a habit of submission and acceptance.

But when examined, the complaints turn out to be in large measure those which are common to all countries where affluence has coincided with some loss of direction. There are also some local sources.

Twenty years of unbroken power for the Liberal–Country Party Coalition have been twenty years in the wilderness for the Labour Party, traditionally, although not alone in this, the party of innovation. During that time, the Labour Party has also been faced with the task of finding new leaders and new programmes, geared to present realities rather than to past shibboleths. This task has provoked struggles for power which have raised all the issues of the relations of the party machine with the party's branches, its parliamentary members, the unions and its intellectuals. In the short-run these disputes have scared the swinging voters and have gone with prosperity to keep Labour's opponents in power. In the long run, they should prove the prelude to a more equal competition between the parties which will stir the voters out of a temporary sluggishness.

In any case, as Dr Robin Gollan has shown in his *Radical and Working Class Politics,* a tension between militant idealism and the necessary compromises of practising politicians is built into the structure of the Labour Party which, in addition to its assured trade union support, must woo the necessary votes of non-unionists if it is to gain power. Vigorous debate on Vietnam, or the penal clauses of the Arbitration Act which employers regard as an indispensable sanction, and the unions as a threat to their right to strike, or on education and social services, have been shaping policies nearer to present circumstances.

Nor have Labour's opponents been without their own soul-searching; and indeed the necessity to devise policies to meet new situations in trade and defence has done something, if not enough, to counter the temptations of prolonged power to complacency. In short, Australian political life may be expected to display some revival of vigour.

Nor is it clear that the charges of unoriginality and imitativeness are fully justified. It is true that there has been a widespread and visible aping of many features of American life from the supermarket to Coca-Cola in Australia as elsewhere. But a young country rapidly developing its industrial and trading capacity is bound to be imitative of the longer experiences to be found elsewhere, and intelligent adaptation is not necessarily hostile to originality.

This is not to say that an Australian looking at his own country at the end of the 1960s can rest complacent. There is much to encourage him, for Australia is one of the most stable countries of the world, as overseas investors realize. Its structure of government is firm: its economic growth, though rapid, is soundly based and its stability is protected by vigilant precautions against unhealthy boom conditions or adverse balance of payments. Its industrial relations, although displaying the recurrent tensions of all highly industrialized societies, are not, despite adverse publicity, abnormally troubled.

But affluence brings its own problems, intensified by the high degree of urbanization. Over 80 per cent of Australians live in towns and cities, the larger of which, Sydney and Melbourne, are now growing rapidly from over 2,000,000 inhabitants towards an estimated 5,000,000 at the close of the century. These things produce their obvious problems—snarled traffic, the slaughter of the roads, the loss of quiet and the destruction of natural beauty, not certainly, nor yet generally, replaced by man-made beauty. Obstinate as these problems are, there lurk behind them others which may prove even more difficult to solve, such as the re-training and re-employment of workers displaced by automation and the equipment of the community to use leisure.

And linked with all these things there run the puzzling problems of affluence—youth without purpose, wealth without a tradition of service, the replacement of quiet by noise, beauty by ugliness, in short, a destruction of life. These are not peculiar to Australia, being the accompaniments of the industrial and urban development, which it shares with other countries; and it would be a distortion to present them as the whole truth.

These problems challenge us as they are challenging other societies, and their solutions can be found only in detailed study. But as our society changes so greatly, it is natural that Australians should ask what sort of society they want. The answer of the Australian legend of the 1890s is too simple, although it contained certain elements of genuine humanity, a valuing of personal worth rather than of station, which retain their validity and their value. Indeed, it may well be that modern Australia has no function for 'an Australian legend' which in its time mainly served to free Australians from what has been called 'the cultural cringe', the habit of looking over the shoulder at English modes—unless we need a new Australian legend to free us from a cultural cringe towards the newly fashionable American modes. The answers to our problems must be found in detail and our self-picture emerge from the common values their solutions serve.

But it has been the argument of this book that Australia's political tradition of experimental practicality, rightly understood, may guide us well in meeting these problems which now bring democracy in question. It is no accident that the sense of the strength to be gained from such a tradition has become a frequent theme in modern Australian writing, as in Judith Wright's poem, 'The Bullocky':

> Beside his heavy-shouldered team,
> thirsty with drought and chilled with rain,
> he weathered all the striding years
> till they ran widdershins in his brain:

> Till the long solitary tracks
> etched deeper with each lurching load
> were populous before his eyes
> and fiends and angels used his road.

> All the long straining journey grew
> a mad apocalyptic dream,
> and he old Moses; and the slaves
> his suffering and stubborn team.

> Then in his evening camp beneath
> the half-light pillars of the trees
> he filled the steepled cone of night
> with shouted prayers and prophecies,

> While past the campfire's crimson ring
> the star-struck darkness cupped him round
> and centuries of cattlebells
> rang with their sweet uneasy sound.

Grass is across the wagon-tracks
and plough strikes bone beneath the grass,
and vineyards cover all the slopes
where the dead teams were used to pass.

O vine grow close upon that bone
and hold it with your rooted hand.
The Prophet Moses feeds the grape
and fruitful is the Promised Land.

Meanwhile, the Australian community has grown more complex and more sophisticated. Australians are best known abroad by their young men of action, their cricketers and tennis players and soldiers; but the achievements of Australia's scholars and scientists, writers and artists, if they are less known, are not less worthy of comment. Lack of opportunity and recognition at home forced a disproportionate number of such Australians in the past to seek opportunity abroad, where many of them were better known for their work than for their origins. It is no longer so widely necessary for talented Australians to choose between exile and obscurity, and Australian achievements in science and scholarship, in literature and the arts have demonstrated a new maturity, a coming of age.

Australia has now a mature economy and a strong political tradition. It is now forging an intellectual and artistic culture at least as responsive to its present industrial society as to its pastoral past. That culture is being made by those who are unready merely to take over the intellectual and artistic fashions of a past era. But dissatisfaction is balanced in present Australian writing by that persistent millennial hopefulness which was first bred by migration to a new land. The marriage of disbelief and faith, now moulding a new self-picture, may be represented by A. D. Hope's poem, 'Australia':

A nation of trees, drab green and desolate grey
in the field uniform of modern wars,
darkens her hills: those endless, outstretched paws
of sphinx demolished or stone lion worn away.

They call her a young country, but they lie;
she is the last of lands, the emptiest,
a woman beyond her change of life, a breast
still tender, but within the womb is dry.

She has no gods, no songs, no history:
the emotions and superstitions of younger lands,
her rivers of water drown among inland sands;
only the river of her stupidity

floods her monotonous tribes from Cairns to Perth.
In them at last those ultimate men arrive
who will not boast 'we live' but 'we survive':
a type that will inhabit the dying earth.

And her five cities, like five teeming sores
each drains her: a vast parasite robber state
where second-hand Europeans pullulate
timidly on the edge of alien shores.

Yet there are some like me turn gladly home
from the lush jungle of modern thought, to find
the Arabian desert of the human mind;
hoping, if still from deserts the prophets come,

such savage and scarlet as no green hills dare
springs in this waste, some spirit which escapes
the learned doubt, the chatter of cultured apes
which is called civilization over there.

NOTE ON BOOKS

Articles and reviews in *Historical Studies, Australia,* published twice yearly by the University of Melbourne, will serve as a guide to present historical writing in Australia. The following is a short list of some of the better-known works which treat matters discussed in this volume.

1. INTRODUCTORY

Geoffrey Blainey, *The Tyranny of Distance* (Melbourne, 1966).
C. M. H. Clark, *A Short History of Australia* (London, 1964).
W. K. Hancock, *Australia* (London, 1930).
Douglas Pike, *Australia: The Quiet Continent* (Cambridge, 1962).
A. G. L. Shaw, *The Story of Australia* (London, 1955).
O. Spate, *Australia* (London, 1968).

2. GENERAL

Alex H. Chisholm (editor), *The Australian Encyclopaedia*; ten volumes (Sydney, 1958).
Cambridge History of the British Empire, vol. VII, Part I, *Australia* (Cambridge, 1933).
T. A. Coghlan, *Labour and Industry in Australia*; 4 vols. (Oxford, 1918). A pioneer work of wide scope; indispensable in the study of Australian history.
B. C. Fitzpatrick, *British Imperialism and Australia, 1783-1833* (London, 1939) and *The British Empire in Australia. An Economic History, 1834-1939* (Melbourne, 1941). Controversial and indispensable.

3. DOCUMENTS

The Historical Records of Australia (Sydney). These are incomplete. Series I consists of twenty-six volumes of governors' dispatches to and from England, 1788-1848. Series III consists of six volumes covering settlements in the different colonies, 1803-29; Series IV has one volume of legal papers, 1786-1827.

C. M. H. Clark, *Select Documents in Australian History, 1788–1850* (Sydney, 1950); *1851–1900* (Sydney, 1955).
M. Clark, *Sources of Australian History* (World's Classics, 1957).

4. THE LAND

The best short introduction is *The Australian Environment*, issued by the Commonwealth Scientific and Industrial Research Organization for the British Commonwealth Agricultural Conference held in Australia, August 1949. (Revised edition, Melbourne, 1960.)
Griffith Taylor, *Australia; A Study of Warm Environments and their Effect on British Settlement* (London, 1940).

5. THE ABORIGINES

The best introduction is the article, 'Aborigines', in *The Australian Encyclopaedia* (see 2. above). See also A. P. Elkin, *The Australian Aborigines: How to Understand Them* (Sydney and London, 1938). Two short special studies of high literary quality which incidentally give an excellent introduction to aboriginal life are T. G. H. Strehlow, *Aranda Traditions* (Melbourne, 1947), and D. H. Thomson, *Economic Structure and the Ceremonial Exchange Cycle in Arnhem Land* (Melbourne, 1949). The massive pioneering works of Baldwin Spencer and F. J. Gillen remain classics of the subject. For continuing studies, see publications of The Australian Institute of Aboriginal Studies, Canberra. For Australian prehistory, see J. D. Mulvaney, *The Prehistory of Australia* (London, 1969).

6. AUSTRALIAN HISTORY TO 1850

The most challenging studies of these early years are the two volumes so far published of C. M. H. Clark's *A History of Australia* (Melbourne, 1962 and 1968). On the penal colonization of Australia, see E. O'Brien, *The Foundation of Australia, 1786–1800* (Sydney, 1950), A. G. L. Shaw, *Convicts and the Colonies. A Study of Penal Transportation . . .* (London, 1966), and L. Lloyd Robson, *The Convict Settlers of Australia* (Melbourne, 1965). On colonial history in the context of British policy in the Pacific, see J. M. Ward, *British Policy in the South Pacific, 1786–1893* (Sydney, 1948). For early colonial society and the position of the governors, see M. H. Ellis, *Lachlan Macquarie* (Sydney, 1947), and Kathleen Fitzpatrick, *Sir John Franklin in Tasmania, 1837–43* (Melbourne, 1949). For Western Australia, see F. K. Crowley, *A Short History of Western Australia* (Melbourne, 1959), and for South Australia, Douglas Pike, *Paradise of Dissent* (London, 1957). The best account of early pastoral society is Margaret Kiddle, *Men of Yesterday. A Social History of the Western District of Victoria, 1834–1890* (Melbourne,

1961). See also S. H. Roberts, *The Squatting Age in Australia, 1835–47* (Melbourne, 1935). For early immigration, see R. B. Madgwick, *Immigration into Eastern Australia, 1788–1851* (London, 1937), and for early government, A. C. V. Melbourne, *Early Constitutional Development in Australia; New South Wales, 1788–1856* (London, 1934).

7. AUSTRALIAN HISTORY, 1850–1900

See works listed in 1. and 2. above. For the gold rushes, see A. G. Serle, *The Golden Age. A History of the Colony of Victoria, 1851–1861* (Melbourne, 1963). For economic development the most important studies are those of N. G. Butlin, particularly *Investment in Australian Development, 1861–1900* (Cambridge, 1964). For political economy, see J. A. La Nauze, *Political Economy in Australia. Historical Studies* (Melbourne, 1949). The same author's *Alfred Deakin. A Biography* (Melbourne, 1965; 2 vols.) is a major study of one of the most important figures in Australian politics before and after 1900. For parliamentary history, see P. Loveday and A. W. Martin, *Parliament, Factions and Parties* (Melbourne, 1966), and for Labour history, Robin Gollan, *Radical and Working Class Politics* (Melbourne, 1960) and H. V. Evatt, *Australian Labour Leader. The Story of W. A. Holman* (Sydney, 1940). For the problems and story of land settlement, see S. M. Wadham and G. L. Wood, *Land Utilization in Australia* (Melbourne, 1950).

8. THE COMMONWEALTH, 1900–70

In addition to books cited in 1., 2. and 7. above, see L. F. Crisp, *The Parliamentary Government of the Commonwealth of Australia* (Adelaide, 1949), G. Greenwood, *The Future of Australian Federalism* (Melbourne, 1946), Geoffrey Sawer, *Australian Federal Politics and Law, 1901–1929* (Melbourne, 1956), L. F. Fitzhardinge, *William Morris Hughes* (Sydney, 1964), the volumes of the official history of Australia in the war of 1914–18 edited by C. E. W. Bean, and of Australia in the war of 1939–45 edited by Gavin Long, J. G. Crawford, *Australian Trade Policy, 1942–66; A Documentary History* (Canberra, 1968), *The Report of the Committee of Economic Enquiry* ('Vernon Committee': 2 vols., Canberra, 1965), and G. Greenwood and N. D. Harper (editors), *Australia in World Affairs, 1956–60* (Melbourne, 1963). See also articles in *Politics and History* published by the University of Queensland.

9. LITERATURE AND THE ARTS

The fullest account of Australian writing is H. M. Green, *A History of Australian Literature, Pure and Applied* (2 vols., Sydney, 1961). There are many studies of Australian architecture. See Robin Boyd, *Australia's Home* (Melbourne, 1952) and *The Australian Ugliness* (Melbourne,

1960) for the views of a prominent architect. On Australian painting, see Bernard Smith, *Place, Taste and Tradition. A Study of Australian Art since 1788* (Sydney, 1945), *European Vision and the South Pacific, 1768–1850* (Oxford, 1960) and *Australian Painting, 1788–1960* (Oxford, 1962).

INDEX